W9-AOV-769

Sally Ann
and the School Show

CHILDREN'S ROOM
Public Library
South Bend, Indiana

Sally Ann
and the School Show

By TERRANCE DICKS

Illustrated by BLANCHE SIMS

PUBLIC LIBRARY

APR 13 1993

SOUTH BEND, INDIANA

SIMON & SCHUSTER BOOKS FOR YOUNG READERS
Published by Simon & Schuster
New York · London · Toronto · Sydney · Tokyo · Singapore

SIMON & SCHUSTER BOOKS FOR YOUNG READERS
Simon & Schuster Building, Rockefeller Center
1230 Avenue of the Americas, New York, New York 10020
Text copyright © 1988 by Terrance Dicks
Illustrations copyright © 1992 by Blanche Sims
All rights reserved including the right of reproduction
in whole or in part in any form.
Originally published in Great Britain by Piccadilly Press Ltd. as
SALLY ANN AND THE SCHOOL PLAY.
SIMON & SCHUSTER BOOKS FOR YOUNG READERS
is a trademark of Simon & Schuster.

Designed by David Neuhaus
Manufactured in the United States of America
10 9 8 7 6 5 4 3 2 1

Library of Congress Cataloging-in-Publication Data
Dicks, Terrance.
Sally Ann and the school show / Terrance Dicks; illustrated by
Blanche Sims.
    p.   cm.
Summary: Sally Ann and the other dolls help Mrs. Foster raise
enough money to keep the day care center open.
[1. Dolls—Fiction.   2. Toys—Fiction.   3. Day Care centers—
Fiction.   4. Moneymaking projects—Fiction.]   I. Sims, Blanche,
ill.   II. Title.
PZ7.D5627Sai   1991
[E]—dc20   91-15418   CIP

ISBN: 0-671-74513-1

Middle Grades   CR
cks, Terrance.
lly Ann and the school
how

Contents

Sally Ann
and the School Show

1

Splash!

It was the end of a long hard day at Mrs. Foster's day care center.

The last children had been called for by their mothers and fathers. The big playroom had been cleaned up. The toys had been put back in the closet—all except one, a rag doll called Sally Ann. She had somehow ended up on the kitchen table.

In the kitchen Mrs. Foster and her helper were having coffee.

"Quite a good day today," said Mrs. Foster happily. She was a plump, kindly lady with straggly gray-brown hair. She wore big round glasses which she kept fastened to a chain around her neck so she wouldn't lose them.

Mrs. Foster was a bit of a scatter-brain.

Her helper, a big, jolly young woman called Sue, took a sip of her coffee. "That's right—and for once nothing seemed to go wrong!"

She ought to have knocked on wood or crossed her fingers or something, because at that very moment things were going very wrong indeed. And only Sally Ann could see it!

That was because of her position—

flat on her back on the table, staring straight up at the ceiling.

Something strange was happening on that ceiling.

Around the part where the light bulb was hanging from the ceiling the white plaster was beginning to turn darker. A little dark circle grew steadily larger.

A circle of dampness!

Suddenly big drops of water began appearing on the wet area. They gathered together in a sort of upside-down pool. Then the water began running down the wire and dripping down from the light bulb—dripping onto Sally Ann's face!

It took all Sally Ann's self-control not to jump up with a yell. Like most toys, she could come to life when she wanted to. But toys aren't supposed to come alive where humans can see them. It's against the rules.

A second drop, then a third splashed onto Sally Ann's face. She was just about to jump up and yell, rules or no rules, when something else happened.

Electricity and water don't mix, and suddenly the light bulb exploded in a shower of sparks. The whole room went dark. Sally Ann rolled over, dropped off the table, and hid underneath it for safety.

"The faucet!" screamed Mrs. Foster. "I left the faucet on in the sink upstairs. I forgot all about it—and the bathroom's just above us."

Sally Ann heard Sue's calm, reassuring voice. "Well, you'd better go and turn it off, then. Wait, there are some candles in the closet."

After a bit of bumping around, there was the scrape of a match. Soon the room was lit by the faint glow of first one and then another flickering candle.

"That's better," said Sue. "Now, you go and see to that faucet, Mrs. Foster, and I'll see if I can fix the lights. Where's the fuse box?"

Sue was very practical.

Mrs. Foster went upstairs and turned off the faucet. She returned a few minutes later more upset than ever. "The

whole bathroom's flooded now. How are you managing with the lights, Sue?"

"Not too well, I'm afraid. I've

changed the fuse and it ought to be all right, but it's not! There must be something else wrong."

"Oh, dear, oh, dear," said Mrs. Foster, in a real panic by now. "It gets dark by suppertime at this time of year. I can't run the center without lights."

Practical as ever, Sue said, "Look, Mr. Klagg's electrical shop is just down the street, and he'll be closing any minute. I'll stop in on my way home and ask him to come by and give you a hand." Sue hurried off.

Sally Ann came out from under the table and climbed up onto a chair. She was determined to wait and see what would happen. She thought she might as well be comfortable. Of course, no one could see her moving in the dark.

Before long Mr. Klagg arrived with

his toolbox and an enormous flashlight. He was a little bald man with wire-framed glasses and a scrubby white mustache. He knew the day care center well. His granddaughter Katy attended and he often brought her and picked her up.

"Don't worry, Mrs. Foster," he said cheerily. "I'll soon get those fuses fixed properly for you. Now, where's the fuse box?"

Mrs. Foster told him where it was in the hall. He trotted off.

Sure enough the lights came on a minute or two later. Sue had already put a new bulb in to replace the broken one.

But when Mr. Klagg came back into the kitchen, his face was sad. "I'm afraid I've got bad news for you, Mrs. Foster."

"What's the matter? You've fixed things, haven't you?"

"Oh, I've fixed things," said Mr. Klagg in a gloomy voice. "But how long's it going to last?"

He went on to explain that some of the electrical wiring in Mrs. Foster's big old house was in a terrible state.

"This kitchen wiring is practically prehistoric. It can't have been touched for years. Most of it'll have to be replaced. Cost you a bundle, I'm afraid."

Mrs. Foster gasped. "How much?"

Mr. Klagg made a sort of sucking noise through his teeth. "Well, you won't see much change out of three hundred dollars. . . ."

Mrs. Foster gasped. "Three hundred dollars."

"'Fraid so. I'll come over tomorrow and give you a more accurate estimate." He paused on the way out.

"Thing is, Mrs. F., the job's got to be

done. That temporary repair will hold for a while. But sooner or later you'll have trouble again. There could even be a risk of fire."

He went off, leaving poor Mrs. Foster in a state of collapse. The trouble was that her little day care center wasn't really a money-making operation. She kept her fees low so that all the working parents around could afford to use it. Each week she just about managed to get by. There was certainly never any spare money. Three hundred dollars was a fortune to her.

Sadly Mrs. Foster poured herself another cup of coffee. "I'll never be able to find three hundred dollars," she said to herself. "I'll have to close down the school. What can I do?"

Although she didn't expect an

answer, she got one all the same. "Non-sense!" said Sally Ann. "If we need the money, we'll just have to get it some-where. There's always a way if you try!"

2

Sally Ann Makes Another Plan

Mrs. Foster peered at the little rag doll. Sally Ann was sitting bolt upright on her chair, arms folded.

"It's all very well saying that, Sally Ann. But how?"

Mrs. Foster was too upset to see anything odd about the fact that she was discussing her problems with a rag doll. Besides, she'd seen Sally Ann come to life before, though in her scatterbrained way she'd almost forgotten about it.

Sally Ann sighed. She could never understand why so many people just gave up when they had a problem. Anyone could see that just sitting around moaning wasn't going to help.

Sally Ann firmly believed that there always was an answer as long as you looked hard enough and didn't give up too soon. Even now a plan was popping into her head.

"People raise money all the time," she said. "They have to these days." She remembered hearing some of the older children talking about their school. Mrs. Foster ran an after-school club for children whose parents wouldn't be home from work when school was over.

Sally Ann said, "The local primary

school is always raising money. They raised hundreds of dollars for new computers not long ago. If they can do it, so can you!"

"But how?" asked Mrs. Foster again. "What do they do?"

"They have events," said Sally Ann. "School fairs, school plays, rummage sales, raffles . . ."

"But which one should we have?"

Sally Ann thought hard. "Well, time's a bit short and you need a lot of money, so we'd better have all of them!"

"What, all at once?"

"Why not?" said Sally Ann. "We'll have a school fair next Saturday. The rummage sale and the raffle can be part of the fair. You can put on some kind of concert or play at the end."

Sally Ann looked at the calendar on

the wall. "Today's Monday, so we've got four days to set it all up. Five if you count the rest of today."

"You mean we're going to start now?" said Mrs. Foster weakly.

Sally Ann quoted one of her favorite sayings. "If not now—when?" She jumped down from her chair. "We'll get started right away, planning it all. You'd better get a pen and paper so you can start taking some notes!"

Meekly Mrs. Foster went over to the little desk in the corner of the kitchen.

That night, when Mrs. Foster was deep in an exhausted sleep, worn out by Sally Ann's stream of instructions, the rest of the toys came to life as usual. Sally Ann told them what she'd done.

As usual, they were horrified at her

nerve—at least at the start. "You really are too much, Sally Ann," said a very pretty doll called Stella. She had long blond hair and could flutter her eyelashes. As far as Sally Ann was concerned, that was about all she was good for.

"Oh, don't be so stuffy, Stella!"

Clarence the gray velvet elephant said sadly, "You *have* broken the rules, you know, Sally Ann!"

"Yess," hissed Kaa. He was a green velvet python with black button eyes. "And not for the firssst time!"

"It was necessary then, and it's necessary now," said Sally Ann.

Jacko the skinny little monkey in the red satin vest gave a roll on his drum. "Hurrah for Sally Ann!"

Arthur the fat teddy bear stuck up for

Sally Ann as well. "I think Sally Ann was right. Think what might happen to us if the center had to close. None of us is new, you know. We might never find new owners!"

There was a little silence as they all thought this over. To be shut away somewhere and never played with is the worst thing that can happen to a toy.

Clarence shuddered. "I think Sally Ann was right to try to help. Is there anything we can do, Sally Ann?"

Sally Ann shook her head. "I don't think so, thanks very much. I've just got to chase Mrs. Foster and see that she keeps chasing everyone else. We've got only a few days to organize everything. . . ."

The next day Mrs. Foster met with her helpers and the children and explained her plan. It was Sally Ann's plan, really, but of course Mrs. Foster couldn't say that.

Everybody got busy right away. All the children started making invitations to the school fair next Saturday. As they were finished, Mrs. Foster copied them on the old duplicator. At the end of the

day every child had a couple of dozen smudgy invitations to take home for family and friends.

Mrs. Foster did a separate leaflet herself, asking for contributions to the rummage sale and helpers to run it. All the mothers or fathers got one when they called for their child.

Mrs. Foster sent Sue out to buy some books of raffle tickets so everyone would have a book of raffle tickets to take home as well.

Last, and most important of all, Sue started holding auditions for the play.

Actually, it turned out it was going to be more of a show than a play. However, three children did agree to perform a play about George Washington and the cherry tree.

Other children agreed to sing songs,

recite poems, or play instruments. A boy named Tom said he'd do magic tricks.

Mrs. Foster was busy all day, making plans and giving instructions. Everyone said what a fine organizer she'd turned out to be.

But whenever things got really tricky, she'd retire to the kitchen "for a quiet think." And she always took Sally Ann with her. When they came back the problem would usually be solved.

At the end of the day it looked as if everything was well underway. And they still had three whole days to set everything up.

Sally Ann didn't know it, but there were still some problems in store for her. The first was a mutiny among her fellow toys. . . .

3

Trouble from the Toys

"It's just not fair, Sally Ann," grumbled Clarence the elephant.

"That's right," said Stella. "We all agree!"

"Yesss," hissed Kaa. "It iss all mosssst unsssatisssfactory!"

Sally Ann surveyed them, hands on hips.

"What's not fair? I've been doing all

the work, trying to save the nursery for you—"

"That's just it," rumbled Arthur the teddy bear. "You're the one who's in the middle of things, having all the fun. We just sit and watch. We're all feeling left out!"

"We all want to help, help, help!" said Jacko, giving a roll on his drum.

For a moment Sally Ann felt angry. She was the one who'd done things and been criticized for it. Now the others were whining at her.

But Sally Ann was kindhearted as well as efficient. And she was a great believer in trying to see the other person's point of view.

"I really don't see how you can help now," she said gently. "Everything is pretty well underway. But I'll tell you what you can do!"

"What's that, Sally Ann?" asked Jacko eagerly.

"You can have a show of your own! After the children's show is over, we'll have one right here. And you guys can do it all. I won't interfere. I'll just sit here and be the audience."

There was a buzz of excitement from all the toys.

"I can sing a little song!" announced Stella. "And I can dance!"

"I can sing too," said Clarence. "I'm a basso profundo, I am!" And he began to rumble a few lines of a song called "Asleep in the Deep." His voice was so deep that it rattled the windows.

"I shall perform my ssspecial messs-merizzzing dance!" hissed Kaa. "You will all be abssolutely fassssscinated!"

"That's the spirit," said Sally Ann. "I'll leave you all to work it out, then."

And she slipped away to have another conference with Mrs. Foster.

Humans and toys alike worked hard during the next few days. All the invitations and appeals for help were distributed. Lots of rummage was sent in and lots of raffle tickets were sold.

There was a moment of panic when they realized they didn't have a prize for the raffle. But Mrs. Foster bravely agreed to sacrifice one of her few pieces of jewelry, a very nice pair of earrings she'd had for years. The liquor store donated wine for the other prizes, and the bakery promised to provide a huge cake. (Both the liquor store lady and the bakery lady had children in the school.)

Friday night seemed to come around with amazing speed. When everyone had gone home, Mrs. Foster and Sally Ann had a last-minute conference in the kitchen.

"We've got lots and lots of rummage," said Mrs. Foster. "Some really nice things too. Some of the moms and dads are coming early in the morning to set up the tables. The raffle tickets are all sold out. The show is a complete sell-out as well!"

"Who's going to be in the show?" asked Sally Ann. "I haven't kept up with that."

"Sue's organized it all," said Mrs. Foster. "It sounds as if it's going to be quite good. Sue says some of the acts are a bit sketchy, so she's putting those on first. But she says she's got three really good ones for the top of the bill. Melanie has been going to ballet classes, so she's a good dancer. Apparently Tom's magic act is good enough to be professional.

"And then, of course, there's Gareth — Gareth the golden voice, Sue calls him. He sings in the school choir. Sue says he's just as good as that boy who used to be on the radio and TV all the time. Sue says that Gareth singing 'God Bless

America' is going to bring the house down. . . . She says that with three really good acts for the top of the bill, we'll get away with the others."

When Sally Ann went back into the playroom that night, she heard snatches of song and music. Then a lot of shuffling and muttering. And then a sudden silence.

By the time she reached the toy closet, all the toys were sitting down, innocently gazing into space.

"All right, all right," said Sally Ann, "I know you've all been rehearsing for your precious show. I wasn't trying to spy on you!"

"It's just that we all want to surprise you, Sally Ann," said Clarence the elephant. "Though I say it myself, it is going to be very good. I'd no idea we were all so talented. What with my singing . . ."

"And mine," said Stella. "And my dance."

"My dance isss ssspectacular!" hissed Kaa.

"Don't tell her all about it, then," rumbled Arthur the teddy bear. "It's going to be a surprise, remember!"

"I really am looking forward to it," said Sally Ann. "And you'll all be able to see the children's show too, you know. We're having it right here. There'll be a little stage and curtains at the far end of the room. Then, when that show's over and everyone's gone home, I'll sit and enjoy yours. I'm sure it'll be much better!"

Sally Ann was awake bright and early

the next morning. She pulled back the
edge of the curtain and let in a shaft of
sunlight.

Perfect! she thought. A nice crisp day, just what we need!

The rummage sale and school fair were going to be held in the big rambling backyard. Then just as it began to get dark, everyone would go inside for the grand finale — the show.

Well, thought Sally Ann, this is it! If only nothing goes wrong.

But of course something did go wrong.

In fact, three somethings!

At the very last minute it looked as if triumph was going to turn into disaster.

It happened like this. . . .

4

The Show Must Go On

At the beginning everything went like a dream.

Everyone worked hard all morning setting things up. In the afternoon they were ready to open, bang, on time.

From then on it was all systems go. People just streamed in. Mothers and fathers, uncles and aunts, grandmothers and grandfathers, all wanting to have a good time.

The rummage sale sold out, and the refreshments nearly sold out. The game booths that the fathers had set up—rolling pennies down a board, knocking cans off a shelf, twenty-one and under at darts, and so on, were busy all the time. The Gypsy fortune-teller—really Mrs. Millet the cleaning lady in a turban—had a long line outside her tent.

Everyone was sorry when the fair was over. But they all filed happily into the big playroom, now set up like a theater, looking forward to the show.

Before long they were all sitting down waiting for the show to start.

And waiting and waiting . . .

Mrs. Foster started to get worried. Still carrying Sally Ann (she'd been clutching her like a mascot all day long), she went out into the kitchen. Sue was surrounded by a group of children, most of them near tears.

"What's happening?" asked Mrs. Foster. "When's the concert going to start? The audience is getting impatient."

"There isn't going to be a show if you ask me," said Sue.

"Why not? What's happened?"

"My top three acts have all gone bad on me," said Sue. "We've got nobody for the top of the bill."

She pointed to the tearful little girl next to her. "Melanie here's been practicing so hard, she's pulled a muscle. She can't walk, let alone dance."

She turned to a shamefaced-looking boy with a huge bandage around his thumb. "Tom's rabbit got tired of being taken out of a hat, turned wild, and bit him. Now any of the old sleight of hand's out of the question."

"Well, there's still Gareth, isn't there?" asked Mrs. Foster hopefully. "You said yourself he was the real star."

Sue turned to Gareth, who was standing beside her in his choirboy's outfit, scowling fiercely.

"Sing, Gareth!" she ordered.

Gareth drew a deep breath, and produced a sound like water gurgling down a rusty drainpipe.

"Oh, no," said Mrs. Foster.

"Oh, yes," said Sue gloomily. "His voice has changed." The trouble with boy sopranos is they stay sopranos for only a short time. And unfortunately, Gareth's voice had changed early.

"Without these three, we just haven't got a show," said Sue. "We'll have to cancel and give back all the ticket money."

"We can't do that," said Mrs. Foster.

"I've been keeping a tally of the takings. We need the money to make up the amount for the electrical work. And besides, it's been such a happy and successful day, I'd hate to send people home disappointed."

"You'll send 'em home in a rage if you charge good money for the acts I've got left," said Sue bluntly.

"Oh, dear, oh, dear," said Mrs. Foster. "Perhaps you're right. Maybe you'd better tell them the show's canceled."

She became aware of a little voice hissing in her ear. "Don't you dare! Just tell Sue to go and start the show. I've got an idea!"

Mrs. Foster did as she was told. Astonished, Sue went to start the show, bustling the children ahead of her.

"Tell Tom to stay," whispered Sally Ann. Mrs. Foster called Tom back.

"Right," said Sally Ann. "Here's what I want him to do. He's to get all the toys and bring them backstage."

A few minutes later Sally Ann was talking to an astonished group of toys in the little backstage area behind the curtain. On the other side of the curtain a nervous little boy named Neal was stumbling through Kipling's famous poem "If" with lots of help from his mother, who was in the front row.

"Now, listen," said Sally Ann. "You all said you wanted to be involved. Here's your chance." She explained what she wanted them to do.

The toys were horrified. "We can't," protested Clarence. "You're asking us all to break the rules."

"It's to save the day care center, isn't it?" said Sally Ann fiercely. "Besides, the way I plan to do it, no one will ever know that the rules have been broken."

It took a lot more talking, but she convinced them at last.

Neal stumbled to the end of his poem. He was replaced by an even more nervous little boy named Jason, scraping away on his violin.

The audience was getting restless. If they didn't get some better entertainment soon, there'd be trouble.

Tom came back with a few more toys.

Sally Ann decided she'd have to let him in on the secret. "Over here," she called.

Tom looked down at her in amazement. "You can talk!"

"That's right. I talk and you listen. You've got to help me save the show, Tom. Here's what we're going to do. . . ."

The violinist finished at last, to everyone's relief. Two little boys and a little girl came on to perform their play about George Washington and the cherry tree. It seemed to go on forever. It wasn't helped by the fact that they were all so nervous they mumbled, and you couldn't hear a word.

By the time the children finished, the audience was getting really fidgety.

Tom took a deep breath and went onstage.

"Ladies and gentlemen, a change in

the program. I proudly present Mrs. Foster's Toy Theater!"

The lights dimmed, so that finally there was just a small bright circle in the center of the stage.

Tom reached out and put Stella into the center of the spotlight.

To everyone's astonishment, Stella stood and sang "Pale Hands I Love," in a sweet, clear little voice. Then she did a quaint little dance, and stood, curtsying, to a storm of applause.

Tom lifted her off the stage and put Jacko and Arthur the teddy bear into the circle of light. Arthur danced a nimble hornpipe while Jacko accompanied him on drum and penny whistle.

Clarence the elephant appeared next and sang "Asleep in the Deep" in a very deep voice indeed.

An owl named Mortimer and a

stuffed lion named Albert sang a duet from a Gilbert and Sullivan operetta. Finally Kaa the snake performed his amazing hypnotic dance, nearly sending several of the audience into trances.

Each act was received with wild applause. Then the lights went down,

and came up a moment later to show all the toys, and Sally Ann too, lined up to take a bow.

They bowed and waved and curtsied. The lights went down again—and the show was over.

Sue and Tom and Mrs. Foster gath-

ered up all the toys and bundled them back in the closet.

People gathered around after the show, congratulating Tom. "Best puppet work I've ever seen, young man," someone said. "How did they do it, Mrs. Foster?"

"Oh, it's just something the children worked out," said Mrs. Foster. "They kept it secret even from me."

"And me," muttered Tom, still hardly able to believe he'd been bossed around by a rag doll. But he accepted all the praise and didn't say anything.

People were talking about the show for a long time afterward. Some people said it was done with invisible strings. Some said a man in a black suit, invisible in the darkness, was moving the toys.

When all the humans had left and

gone to bed, there was a celebration in
the playroom.

Sally Ann had persuaded Mrs. Foster
to leave out the leftover cakes and lem-
onade. There wasn't much, but it was
enough for the toys. They had a wonder-
ful party.

Finally Arthur the teddy bear held up his paw. "Ladies and gentlemen, I give you Sally Ann. What would we do without her?"

"Sally Ann!" cried all the toys, raising their glasses in salute.

And for once, Sally Ann was at a loss
for words!

About the author

After editing scripts for the *Doctor Who* television series for six years, Terrance Dicks went on to write fifty Doctor Who books based on the program. In addition he has fifty children's books to his credit, including the Goliath series.

In recent years he has worked as a script editor and producer for the BBC Classic Serial.

Mr. Dicks lives in London.

About the illustrator

Blanche Sims has illustrated many books for children, including all the titles in the Kids of the Polk Street School Series by Patricia Reilly Giff, *Joey's Head* by Gladys Cretan, and *Sally Ann on Her Own* by Terrance Dicks.

Blanche Sims lives in Westport, Connecticut.

j Middle Grades   CR
Dicks, Terrance.
Sally Ann and the school
 show

WITHDRAWN

DECISION MAKING IN THE SUPREME COURT OF THE UNITED STATES

A Political and Behavioral View

Joseph F. Menez

UNIVERSITY PRESS OF AMERICA

LANHAM • NEW YORK • LONDON

Copyright © 1984 by

University Press of America,™ Inc.

4720 Boston Way
Lanham, MD 20706

3 Henrietta Street
London WC2E 8LU England

All rights reserved

Printed in the United States of America

Library of Congress Cataloging in Publication Data

Menez, Joseph Francis, 1917-
  Decision making in the Supreme Court of the United
States.

  Bibliography: p.
  Includes index.
  1. United States. Supreme Court. 2. Judicial process
—United States. I. Title.
  KF8742.M45 1984   347.73'26   84-5176
  ISBN 0-8191-3948-3 (alk. paper)   347.30735
  ISBN 0-8191-3949-1 (pbk. : alk. paper)

All University Press of America books are produced on acid-free
paper which exceeds the minimum standards set by the National
Historical Publications and Records Commission.

For Charlene

With Love and Admiration

TABLE OF CONTENTS

PREFACE

In a rudimentary form, this Essay was initially written as an undocumented "entertainment" when I was finishing a different work. Summaries of Leading Cases on the Constitution. After what some of my students in constitutional law and some of my colleagues had to say about it, I then rewrote the Essay--I dare not call this slender volume a book - and included my authorities. The Essay pretends to be no more than a brief discussion of the decisionist process of the Supreme Court. It leans heavily on established scholars - those whose works I have read and consulted and those who generously gave me their time and answered my questions. The Essay, I believe, can be read nicely enough without consulting the footnotes - certainly, not all of them. I lean in that direction myself. If, however, one is willing to interrupt the narrative, he will, I am sure, find the authorities and discussions useful.

In writing this Essay, I wanted to clarify for constitutional law students - especially those under-graduates in political science as well as the general reader who has an interest in judicial procedure and behavior - the Supreme Court process and practice. The Court might possess neither the purse nor the sword. It does possess, however, a good deal of mystique. So much attention is given to cases, briefing them, locating "the holding" and the like that the Supreme Court as a small decisionist group often escapes notice. The Bretheren who have risen to the very top of their profession deserve something better than that kind of sterile scrutiny. For the undergraduate political science student, constitutional law is and has to be different from law school constitutional law in that the for the former there is more attention to politics and psychology, dissents and learned social science journals, than the latter which is concerned with the current law.

I want to thank my students in constitutional law who always bring forth fresh views and insights to some old - and not so old - Supreme Court issues. I owe a good deal of my own thinking to my luncheon friends - "the Alexis de Tocqueville coterie" - for their stimulating discussions. Professors John Cranor, Raymond Scheele, S. J. Vasicko, Roger Hollands, and Gary Crawley saved me more than once from political and constitutional quicksand by putting their knowledge of constitutional politics at my disposal. Professor

Richard A. Matre, Department of History, Loyola
University, Chicago, but now Provost for the Medical
Center, was always generous in developing historical
continuities for me. I fondly recall how we "sat out"
the Presidential election of 1980 and the Congressional
elections of 1982 with our wives in Peniche, Portugal,
and despite the very meager news available, we "debated"
the work of the Court. Herbert Hamilton, Professor
Emeritus of constitutional law, Ball State University
and a member of the Delaware County Bar Association,
read the entire manuscript and offered valuable suggestions. He is a thoughtful colleague. Dr. Sally Jo
Vasicko, Chairman of the Department of Political Science,
kindly arranged my teaching schedule so that I could
have uninterrupted research time. I am grateful to her
and the previous chairman, Raymond Scheele, for offering
me some department funds for early typing expenses.
Mrs. Norma C. Wells typed the final manuscript and
neatly unscrambled my handwritten "additions." More
than a typist, she also saved me from some errors.
Mrs. Madonna Checkeye, Department Secretary, and
Mrs. Normajean Reavis, Office Assistant, helped in
untold ways. Affable and always willing to help they
succeeded in reducing or eliminating a good deal of
minutiae. At one time or another when visiting my
children in Texas, Hawaii, and Chicago, I tested my
views with my sons, Michael and Martin Menez and my
daughter Mary and son-in-law, Michael Kearns. I learned
to value their views and insights. Lastly, I want to
acknowledge that my wife, Charlene, realized much
earlier than I did that this brief "entertainment" might
grow into a "longish" Essay.

     Needless to say, not all my colleagues who read
this Essay in manuscript form agree with my account of
the Court's inner workings or the conclusions I draw.
I could not expect such an agreement nor did I seek it.
Their comments and suggestions helped me immeasurably
but I am, naturally, solely responsible for errors and
omissions.

DECISION-MAKING IN THE SUPREME COURT OF THE UNITED

STATES: A POLITICAL AND BEHAVIORAL VIEW

CHAPTER I

The Court Views Itself And Does Its Work

"We are under the Constitution," said Chief
Justice Charles Evans Hughes, "but the Constitution is
what the Judges say it is."[1] Justice Felix Frankfurter
was even more blunt. He wrote: "The Supreme Court is
the Constitution."[2] With views such as these, it is no
wonder that despite Alexander Bickel's title for the
Court, The Least Dangerous Branch, others such as Raoul
Berger see it as being less accountable, as "Government
by Judiciary. Both Chief Justice Hughes and Associate
Justice Frankfurter were stretching a point, no doubt,
inasmuch as the Court, as Alexander Hamilton noted in
The Federalist, has "neither force nor will, but merely
judgment."[3] But it is precisely the Court's judgment -
especially when the law itself is unclear - which is
all important, for them as Justice Felix Frankfurter
put it, the Court sits in judgment and "breathes life,
feeble or strong, into the inert pages of the Constitution . . .."[4] We must note, as Alexis de Tocqueville
did in Democracy in America, that "scarcely any political question arises in the United States that is not
resolved, sooner or later, into a judicial question."[5]
Chief Justice Warren Burger was not boasting when he
defined the Court as a "select company not because we
are all knowing, but because we were selected and we
are here."[6]

In analyzing Supreme Court decision-making there
are several discrete "decision-points": thus, the vote
on whether or not to accept a case for discussion, a
vote on its merits, the politics of assignment, and
the content of the majority and minority opinions.
Except when the Court hands down an opinion, it is out
of the public eye, and yet it was Justice Oliver
Wendell Holmes who said: "We are very quiet there, but
it is the quiet of a storm cellar."[7] The recent

1

"reverse discrimination" case illustrates this.[8]

What exacerbates the decisional process is the competing philosophies that motivate the justices. No Justice, not even the most junior, begins with a "clean slate;" and every justice, of course, can be expected to change his mind or alter his viewpoint. "It is hardly the absence of viewpoint or outlook that we seek in a judge; the village idiot would be the most qualified if it were. Rather, it is the style and manner of arriving at, applying, and altering viewpoints that characterizes a judicious mind."[9] If the Justice is an "activist," he would like to see the Court intervene vigorously in the policy-making process, as did Chief Justice Earl Warren who wrote: ". . . the beginning of justice is the capacity to generalize and make objective one's private sense of wrong."[10] If he is a "non-activist" he would like the Court to defer to the elected branches as did John Marshall Harlan who wrote: "The Constitution is not a panacea for every blot upon the public welfare."[11]

Cases come before the Supreme Court in several ways: by certification, by original judisdiction, by certiorari, and by appeal.[12] Certification is a procedure infrequently and rarely used. It permits the Court of Appeals or the Court of Claims to seek further instructions on a point of law. Described as undesirable, virtually obsolete, and concerned with abstract questions of law, nevertheless, it has not yet been repealed "and . . . has been sporadically invoked in recent years."[13] Under original jurisdiction, the Court decides an insignificant number of cases, in fact, only about 140 since the first term of the Court in 1789. Such cases will never have been in the lower courts.[14] These are cases involving disputes between diplomatic officials and between states. Certiorari is a writ addressed by the Court to a lower court calling upon it to "certify" or send up its records. Any four affirmative votes sometimes called the "Rule of Four" - of the Court is sufficient to bring this case up for argument and decision. Certiorari is discretionary. If the petition is denied, that ends the matter inasmuch as the Court never indicates why it refused. To give "reasons" at this stage would be "to try" the issue. An appeal is a constitutional right involving a "federal question." In practice though, the difference between certiorari and appeal hardly exists for the reason that the Court can refuse the latter "for want of a substantial federal question."[15] Despite the

2

statutory guarantee of a Supreme Court review, the Court
has complete discretion and has not spelled out the
meaning of this phrase or explained why a given case
lacks a substantial federal question or why jurisdiction
is found wanting.[16]

For the October Term, 1981 ending July, 1982, the
Court disposed of 167 cases of which 141 were decided
by signed opinions and 26 decided by per curiam
opinions. This is, of course, the public work of the
Court. In its private work it disposes of several
thousand cases, for seldom does the Court have the
time or need to read or even skim through the entire
record. In its final disposition of cases for the
1981-82 term, the Court on its original docket disposed of 6 cases, in its appellate docket 2417 cases
and on its miscellaneous docket 2033 cases for a grand
total of 4456 cases.[17] Justice Brennan noted that 70%
of the cases docketed to be reviewed do not even merit
conference discussion.[18] Even after the Justices have
left Washington during the adjournment period, certiorari petitions follow them in diplomatic pouches.[19]
About 5000 "certs" come before the Court per term.
Most of them are frivolous. Petitions are filed at the
same rate in summer ("vacation") as during the regular
term - some 70 to 80 weekly.[20] Most of the Justices
complain of the unrewarding and time-consuming nature
of "cert". Two recent exceptions are Justice William
O. Douglas[21] and Justice William Brennan, the former
claiming that petitions did not take much time, and
the latter reading all the petitions. Each Justice,
said Brennan, unless he disqualifies himself, "passes
on each petition, each item, no matter how drawn, in
longhand, by typewriter, or on a press."[22] No wonder
that Alexander Bickel, a critic of the Court's appellate burdens, thought that Justice Brennan, on finishing all the petitions, had no time left for anything
else and that Douglas' views were frivolous and
extravagant.[23] By contrast, careful Justice that he
was, Justice Brandeis spent little time in studying
petitions for certiorari. Nor did he use his clerks
on them. If a petition did not make out a clear case
for review, it was denied.[24]

Soon after being named Chief Justice, Harlan F.
Stone was invited to visit England in the summer of
1942 but refused, saying he needed all the rest he
could get in July "before the grind of 'certs'
begins."[25] A possible cause of this "cert" fatigue is
the manner in which Chief Justice Stone differed from

3

Chief Justice Hughes in processing certiorari petitions.
Hughes came to the conference fully prepared, having
read the petitions and weeded out the meritless ones
and allowed about three and one-half minutes for discussion. He was never challenged by the other Justices,
barely tolerated debate, and discouraged requests for
more time to study the matter.[26] By contrast Stone
abandoned the summary disposal practice used by Hughes
and encouraged full discussion and debate. Moreover,
he often presented his own views diffidently, and
"allowed himself to be freely interrupted, and invariably granted extensions" of time.[27] Unlike his great
colleague, Justice Brandeis, time and again Justice
Oliver Wendell Holmes complained of the burden of
certiorari reading. In a letter to Sir Frederick
Pollock, he wrote: "But during the summer hateful mail-
bags of petitions for certiorari will keep coming in.
They are a chore."[28] Theodore Voorhees laments the
diminishing strength Holmes had to spend on "detested"
petitions.[29]

> One thing was true in 1928 as it is
> today. The petitions . . . take an
> inordinate toll of each Justice's time,
> and whether Holmes voted them up or down,
> they left no lasting monument to judicial
> acumen, literary ability, or philosophic
> intellect.[30]

Certiorari petitions escalated under the Warren
Court.[31] Chief Justice Burger called attention to the
fact that in the first term of Warren's tenure
(October, 1953) the Court announced 65 signed opinions,
and in his final term (October, 1968) there were 99.
Between 1953 and 1968 there was an average of 96 signed
opinions, and the average between 1969 and 1977 was
125.[32] In 1937 there were fewer than 1000 new filings
on the Supreme Court docket. In 1962 the number had
increased to 2800, and currently it is about 4000.
"No longer", says Justice White, "is it possible to
review 20% or even 10% of the cases in which petitions
are filed." For 24 years ending in the 1970 Term, in
cases granted plenary consideration, the Court issued
an average of 101 full opinions plus 10 to 15 per
curiam opinions. "Since 1970", the Chief Justice concluded, "we have averaged 132 full opinions plus 15
per curiams - these opinions deciding an average of
170 cases . . ."[33]

"As a new member of the Court," said Justice Lewis

Powell, "I can say without qualification that I find the situation disquieting."[34] By mid-1975, five of the nine Justices had indicated their support for some kind of a national court of appeals, the four Nixon appointees and Justice Bryon White.[35] By contrast, Justices Arthur Goldberg, Potter Stewart, William O. Douglas and Chief Justice Earl Warren labeled the alleged burdens of certiorari petitions as inaccurate and claimed that the "very heavy caseload is neither intolerable nor impossible to handle."[36] Justice William O. Douglas thought it all boiled down to "about a four-day-a-week-job" and the case for "overwork" is a myth,[37] an assessment even his friends did not believe.[38]

Professor Philip Kurland suggested that each Justice have a quota of "certs," and thus each Justice would have to use them prudently.[39] Chief Justice Harlan Stone, who refused to put a limit on "certs," would certainly have chafed under this proposal.[40] To beat the "cert" problem some of the Justices have "spawned an experiment,"[41] combining their clerks and dividing the petitions among the five chambers with the law clerk's memoranda going to each of the five Justices. Although it was pointed out[42] that this was a division of work among the clerks, it was not a consideration of judgment like the consideration among the Justices. In fact, Professor Kurland is incensed that law clerks stand between him and the Justice. "I am resentful of the fact," he wrote, "that my petition will not be read by members of the high court, that they will see only what their law clerks permit them to see."[43]

Additionally, some critics would like the Court to publicly announce that for a given period of time certain categories of cases would no longer be reviewed and that lawyers who prepared frivolous petitions would be professionally chastised. This could be accomplished by publishing the "dead list," that is, those petitions automatically rejected because they could not get even one Justice to support them.[44] Lawyers, of course, confront a dilemma that has resulted from the expansion of individual liberties. A lawyer who does not file a petition to appeal runs the risk of being sued for malpractice. Alexander Bickel, a former law clerk to Justice Frankfurter, objected to law clerks who start out as "assistants" to some Justice and then became "memoranda writers on petitions for review."[45]

In 1972, acting under statutory authority, Chief Justice Burger appointed a distinguished panel of legal

authorities[46] - quickly called the Freund Committee
after its chairman, Paul Freund of the Harvard Law
School - to review the appellate process. The Freund
Committee set off a national debate when it "proposed
the establishment of a new, seven-member court that
would screen all petitions sent to the Supreme Court."[47]
One of the major reasons for creating the Freund Committee on the Court's case load was to cut down the
cases for plenary review that now glut the Court's
docket. The Chief Justice believes the creation of the
proposed National Court of Appeals is imperative.
Despite a considerable body of literature on both sides,
however it has not yet gotten off the ground. The
Chief Justice keeps returning to this necessity[48] as
does Mr. Justice Brennan in opposition.[49]

Defenders of the Court's present appellate flexi-
bility view the proposed National Court of Appeals as
a conservative attempt to stem the Warren Court tide
and as a device to prevent libertarian and civil rights
groups from getting to the Supreme Court. Nathan Lewin
has noted that unlike in the Warren Court era when
civil rights organizations lost in the lower courts but
won in the Warren Court, today appeals are more likely
to be taken by the Attorney General and won.[50]

Libertarians consider the Burger Court hostile to
civil liberties. In fact their strategy currently is
to avoid petitioning the Court and to wait for a change
in the Court's personnel. According to journalist
Nina Totenberg the liberal Justices have an unwritten
agreement to keep civil liberties cases out of the
hands of the conservative majority. The liberals will
vote not to hear a case on appeal "even if it involves
what they consider a horrendous lower court decision"
because they do not want it decided against them,
hoping for a better day and a liberal court.[51] As
Joseph Onek, Director of the Washington Center for Law
and Social Policy said: "There is no question that we
now avoid the Supreme Court."[52] Meanwhile civil rights
organizations have stepped up their work as administrative lobbyists.[53] On the average they know that there
is a court appointment about every twenty-two months[54]
and that the person appointed is ideologically close to
the President. What has captured the attention of the
country in mid-1983 is the upcoming election of 1984.
Will President Reagan seek a second term and whom will
the Democrats nominate? Some attention is given to
Mr. Reagan's age but no attention is given to an already
old Supreme Court. Five of the nine Justices are

74 years old or older. The oldest Justices (Brennan and Marshall) are liberal and the almost liberal, Blackmun, is 74. In addition, none of these justices is in very good health. As a second term President Reagan would be expected to push his social programs strongly and appoint a Court majority to keep them intact if challenged. As a second term President, he might not rival the six appointments of Taft or the five appointments of Eisenhower but he could be expected to appoint enough Justices to make his views felt for some time.[55]

CHAPTER I

[1]Merlo J. Pusey, Charles Evans Hughes (New York: Macmillan Co., 1952), I, p. 204. Chief Justice Charles E. Hughes told Justice William O. Douglas: "You must remember one thing. At the constitutional level where we work, ninety percent of any decision is emotional. The rational part of us supplies the reasons for supporting our predilections." William O. Douglas, The Court Years 1939-1975 (New York: Random House, 1980), p. 8.

[2]Alpheus Thomas Mason, "Myth and Reality in Supreme Court Decisions," 48 Virginia Law Review, 1385, 1397 (1962). "Let us face the fact," he commented bluntly, "that five Justices of the Supreme Court are molders of policy, rather than impersonal vehicles of revealed truth." Ibid.

[3]The Federalist, No. 78, ed. W. J. Ashley (New York: E. P. Dutton, 1934), 396. Alexander M. Bickel, The Least Dangerous Branch: The Supreme Court at the Bar of Politics (Indianapolis: Bobbs-Merrill, 1962). Raoul Berger, Government by Judiciary (Cambridge: Harvard University Press, 1977). Doris Marie Provine, Case Selection in the United States Supreme Court (Chicago: University of Chicago Press, 1980) accurately points out that the Court's case selection discretion enables it to determine to what degree it will become involved with all levels of government and is thus no longer Hamilton's passive institution. p. 2.

[4]Henry J. Abraham, Justices and Presidents: A Political History of Appointments to the Supreme Court (New York: New York University Press, 1974), p. 50.

[5]Alexis de Tocqueville, Democracy in America, ed. by Philips Bradley (New York: Vintage Books, 1945), Vol. 1, p. 290. Archibald Cox, former Solicitor General of the United States, suggests some disturbing questions regarding political losers retreating to the courts to achieve goals denied them in the electoral arena. Archibald Cox, The Role of the Supreme Court in American Government (New York: Oxford University Press, 1976), Chapter two. Erwin N. Griswold, Solicitor General of the United States (1967-1973) raises Cox's point somewhat differently, saying: "I do not think that the public or the bar is fully aware of the extent to which the Supreme Court of the United States has become a civil rights court." Erwin N. Griswold, "Rationing Justice - The Supreme Court's Caseload and What the Court Does Not Do," 60 Cornell Law Review, 343 (1975).

[6]Mary Ann Harrell, Equal Justice Under Law: The Supreme Court in American Life (rev. ed.: Washington, D.C.: The Foundation of the Federal Bar Association, 1975), p. 116. One does not have to believe that all the Justices are "great men" - we know they are not - but a good number are and a number equal to if not surpassing Presidents. Part of "this greatness," says Justice Holmes, is ". . . in his being there." David N. Atkinson, "Minor Supreme Court Justices: Their Characteristics and Importance," 3 Florida State University Law Review 348 (1975).

[7]Merlo J. Pusey, Charles Evans Hughes, II, p. 670.

[8]Regents of the University of California v. Allen Bakke, 438 U.S. 265 (1978).

[9]Samuel Krislov, The Supreme Court in the Political Process (New York: Macmillan Co., 1965), p. 75. For an example of a "clean slate" case see Radovich v. National Football League, 352 U.S. 445, (1957) in which the Court refuses to include baseball under anti-trust given the political climate and adds: "If this ruling is unrealistic, inconsistent, or illogical, it is sufficient to answer . . . that were we considering the question of baseball for the first time upon a clean slate we would have no doubts." See the reasons for judicial policy making in Harold J. Spaeth, Supreme Court Policy: Making Explanations and Predictions (San Francisco: W. H. Freeman, 1979), pp. 8-17. See the perceptive chapter "The Tyranny of Labels" in Philip B. Kurland, Politics, the Constitution, and the Warren Court (Chicago: University of Chicago Press, 1970), pp. 1-20.

[10]Joseph F. Menez, "Whose Judicial Temperament?" Commonweal, April 10, 1959, p. 51. For a discussion of judicial activism, see Henry J. Abraham, The Judicial Process: An Introductory Analysis of the Courts of the United States, England, and France (3rd ed.: New York: Oxford University Press, 1975), pp. 320-328. For an excellent compilation of readings which discusses judicial activism and restraint, see Stephen C. Halpern and Charles M. Lamb (eds), Supreme Court Activism and Restraint (Lexington: Lexington Books, D.C. Heath & Co., 1982). "When . . . Warren bends his bulk over the high bench to ask some prosecutor, defending an appealed conviction with citations and precedents and principles, "yes, yes - but were you fair?" the fairness he refers to is no jurisprudential abstraction." Fred Rodell, "It Is the Earl Warren Court," The New York Times Magazine, March 13, 1966, p. 28. "It is fair to say," says Anthony Lewis, "that he (Warren) did not place high value on doctrinal consistency" and thus his "opinions are difficult to analyze because they are likely to be unanalytical." Anthony Lewis, "A Man Born to Act, Not to Muse" The New York Times Magazine, June 30, 1968, pp. 47-48. See also Anthony Lewis, "Earl Warren," in Leon Friedman and Fred L. Israel, The Justices of the

<u>United States Supreme Court 1789-1969 Their Lives and Major</u>
<u>Opinions</u> (New York: Chelsea House and R. R. Bowker Co., 1969),
IV, pp. 2721-2746. For a useful compilation of cases during the
Warren Court years, see Harold J. Spaeth, <u>The Warren Court: Cases</u>
<u>and Commentary</u> (San Francisco: Chandler Publishing Co., 1966).
For a scholarly compilation of essays on the Warren Court, see
Barry E. Boyer and Robert E. Gooding Jr., <u>The Warren Court: A</u>
<u>Critical Analysis</u> (New York: Chelsea House, 1968). Arthur Goldberg
who left the Supreme Court to become Ambassador to the United
Nations, discusses "judicial activism and strict construction" in
<u>Equal Justice, the Warren Era of the Supreme Court</u> (Evanston:
Northwestern University Press, 1971), pp. 35-36. It must be
mentioned, in all fairness, that the dichotomy of "judicial activism" and "strict construction" is not what the "judicial restraint"
school is defending. Elliot E. Slotnick, "Who Speaks for the
Court? "View from the States" 26 <u>Emory Law Journal</u>, 107 (1977) distinguishes between the behavioralists and constitutional law
scholars with the former concentrating on an analysis of the vote
on the merits and the latter interested in the final product of
that vote. "Behavioralists," he writes, "are often unwilling to
grant a proper place to "the law" in what they see primarily as
the socio-policical acts of adjudication; traditional constitutional
lawyers remain equally culpable of the oposite sin - the tendency
to view the law mechanistically as the product of rigorous legal
analysis and little else." Constitutional scholars, continues
Slotnick, look to the majority opinion as "the law" and all too
often ignore completely dissents and concurrences or, at best,
treat them as "peripheral concerns." Dorothy B. James, "Role
Theory and the Supreme Court," 30 <u>The Journal of Politics</u>, 160
(1968) distinguishes among traditionalists, the realists and the
behavioralists and suggests somewhat amusingly but not incorrectly
that the difference among them recalls the story of the emperor
and his new clothes. "The traditionalists," she writes, "firmly
maintains that the emperor is majestically apparelled. The realist
indignantly asserts that he is stark naked, and hints at infantile
dependence problems for those who require his clothes. The
behavioralist wishes to ascertain why he is not clothed, and con-
structs indices by which one may determine on any given occasion,
the degree of his exposure." Former Justice Arthur Goldberg
argues that the activism of the Warren Court was right and of the
Burger Court which reverses the Warren Court wrong. He writes:
"Stare decisis applies with unequal force - that when the Supreme
Court seeks to overrule in order to cut back the individual's
fundamental, constitutional protections against governmental
interference, the commands of stare decisis are all but absolute;
yet when a Court overrules to expand personal liberties, the
doctrine interposes a markedly less restrictive caution." Quoted
by Charles M. Lamb and Mitchell S. Lustig, "The Burger Court,
Exclusionary Zoning, and the Activist-Restraint Debate," <u>University</u>
<u>of Pittsburg Law Review</u> 40 (1979) reprinted in S. Sidney Ulmer,

Courts, Laws and Judicial Processes (New York: The Free Press, 1981), p. 341.

[11]Reynolds v. Sims, 377 U.S. 533 (1964) Harlan, J., (dissenting). Some other examples of the judicial restraint view: In Colegrove v. Green, 328 U.S. 549 (1946) Justice Frankfurter warned the Court "ought not to enter this political thicket" and if Congress fails to act properly authority for dealing with such problems ultimately lies with the people." Dissenting in Baker v. Carr, 369 U.S. 186, (1962) Frankfurter said: "In a democractic society like ours, relief must come through an aroused popular conscience that sears the conscience of the people's representatives." In San Antonio v. Rodriquez, 411 U.S. 1 (1973) Justice Powell wrote: "But the Constitution does not provide judicial remedies for every social and economic ill." In United States v. Butler, 297 U.S. 1 (1936) Stone, J., (dissenting) wrote: ". . . the only check upon our own exercise of power is our own sense of self-restraint. For the removal of unwise laws from the statute books appeal lies not to the courts but to the ballot and to the processes of democractic government." More recently in the Abortion Decision, Roe v. Wade, 410 U.S. 113 (1973) White, J., (dissenting) wrote: ". . . an exercise of raw judicial power . . . an improvident and extravagant exercise of the power of judicial review." It is the view attributed to Justice Powell that the Court paved the way for eighteen-year-olds that disturbs the judicial restraint advocates. After pointing out that judges are "elected" (by whom?) for life and are not responsible to the people politically yet it must at time make decisions "that the legislative branch may be reluctant to make . . ." It was, he continued, "the Supreme Court that made the difficult decision, one the Congress apparently did not want to make, to lower the voting age to 18. There was nothing in the Constitution that could have suggested that result. In the simplest terms, the Court decided that when young people were being drafted to go to war and risk their lives at age 18, the time had come to extend to them the right to participate as citizens in the decisions that affected them so seriously." Quoted by William F. Buckley, Muncie, Ind. Star, May 8, 1980. For a strong view of the Court as a "legislature" and an equally strong dissent see Geoffrey C. Hazard, "The Supreme Court as a Legislature" 64 Cornell Law Review, 1-27, (1978) and Raoul Berger, "The Supreme Court as a Legislature: A Dissent" 64 Cornell Law Review, 988-999 (1979).

[12]Sheldon Goldman and Thomas P. Jahnige, The Federal Courts as a Political System (New York: Harper and Row, 1971), pp. 30, 32. Henry J. Abraham, The Judiciary: The Supreme Court in the Governmental Process (3rd ed.: Boston: Allyn and Bacon, 1973), p. 26. John E. Nowak, Ronald D. Rotunda, and J. Nelson Young, Handbook of Constitutional Law (St. Paul: West Publishing Co., 1978), p. 32. See Gerald Gunther, Constitutional Law: Cases and Materials (Mineola: The Foundation Press, 1975), pp. 71-75.

[13]Robert L. Stern and Eugene Gressman, Supreme Court Practice (Fifth ed.: Washington: The Bureau of National Affairs, 1978), pp. 69-70. Harold J. Spaeth, Supreme Court Policy Making, p. 41.

[14]Sheldon Goldman and Thomas P. Jahnige, The Federal Courts as a Political System, pp. 29-30. Robert L. Stern and Eugene Gressman, Supreme Court Practice, pp. 601-625.

[15]Harold J. Spaeth, An Introduction to Supreme Court Decision Making (Rev. ed.: New York: Chandler Publishing Co., 1972), p. 17. David W. Rohde and Harold J. Spaeth, Supreme Court Decision Making (San Francisco: W. H. Freeman Co., 1976), p. 119. On dismissal of a writ of certiorari - after oral argument and further study - see Robert L. Stern and Eugene Gressman, Supreme Court Practice, pp. 369-374, 377-378. Erwin N. Griswold, former Solicitor General of the United States (1967-1973), calls attention to "the virtual disappearance of the distinction between certiorari and appeal" and that "there is no practical distinction between appeal and certiorari" and, further, that appeals are now subject to the Rule of Four just as petitions for certiorari. Erwin N. Griswold, "Rationing Justice - The Supreme Court's Caseload and What the Court Does Not Do," 60 Cornell Law Review, 344, 346 (1975). One distinguished authority, the former Assistant Solicitor General of the United States and co-author of the monumental, Supreme Court Practice, Eugene Gressman believes that if current proposals are enacted by Congress, all review will be discretionary by the route of certiorari. See, "Requiem for the Supreme Courts' Obligatory Jurisdiction," 65 American Bar Association Journal, 1325-1329 (September, 1979). However, the legal effects of denial of petitions for certiorari and the dismissal of appeals are different inasmuch as the former is not a legal precedent and the latter is and thus binding on lower courts. Doris M. Provine, Case Selection in the United States Supreme Court, p. 15.

[16]David W. Rohde and Harold J. Spaeth, Supreme Court Decision Making, p. 119.

[17]For complete statistics see 96 Harvard Law Review, 304-311 (1982). For a sophisticated discussion of why the Court grants or denies petitions for certiorari beyond the Court's Rule 19, see Robert L. Stern and Eugene Gressman, Supreme Court Practice, Appendix A, pp. 1073-1116 at 1085. Stern and Gressman are "stars" practicing before the Supreme Court. Stern was formerly Acting Solicitor General of the United States, and Gressman was formerly Law Clerk, Supreme Court of the United States. See Joseph Tanenhaus, Martin Schick, Mathew Muraskin, and Daniel Rosen, "The Supreme Court's Certiorari Jurisdiction: Cue Theory" in Sheldon Goldman and Austin Sarat, American Court Systems: Readings in Judicial Process and Behavior (San Francisco: W. H. Freeman Co., 1978), pp. 130-143. "I think it is safe to say," said Chief

Justice Charles Evans Hughes, "that about 60 percent of the applications for certiorari are wholly without merit . . . I think that it is the view of the members of the Court that if any error is made in dealing with these applications it is on the side of liberality." Robert L. Stern and Eugene Gressman, Supreme Court Practice, p. 258. For an additional discussion of "cue theory" see S.S. Ulmer, William Hintze, and Louise Kirklosky, "The Decision to Grant or Deny Certiorari: Further Considerations of Cue Theory," 6 Law and Society Review 637-643 (1972). Cue theory, of course, maintains that the Justices of the Supreme Court employ cues as a means of separating those petitions worthy of scrutiny from those that may be discarded without further study.

[18]Robert L. Stern and Eugene Gressman, Supreme Court Practice, p. 344.

[19]Richard L. Williams, "Supreme Court of the United States: the Staff That Keeps it Operating," Smithsonian, January, 1977, p. 46. Nina Totenberg, "Conflict at the Court," Washington Magazine, February, 1974, reprinted in Annual Editions, Readings in American Government '77-'78 (The Dushkin Publishing Group, Inc., Sluice Dock, Guilford Ct., 1977), p. 145.

[20]Lewis F. Powell, "Myths and Misconceptions About the Supreme Court," 61 American Bar Association Journal, 1345 (Nov. 1975). The growth of amicus briefs, on occasion, as 24 in the school desegregation cases, 26 in the first "reverse discrimination" case (including one in behalf of sixty law school deans) are causing the Court additional labor. James MacGregor Burns, J. W. Peltason, and Thomas E. Cronin, Government by the People (Englewood Cliffs: Prentice-Hall, Inc., 1975), p. 413. In Regents of the University of California v. Bakke 429 U.S. 953 (1978) some sixty-nine amicus briefs were filed, and in Brown v. Board of Education of Topeka, 347 U.S. 483 (1954) fifty-one filed. Steve Brill, "The Law," Esquire, April 11, 1978, p. 17.

[21]Nina Totenberg, "Behind the Marble, Beneath the Robes," The New York Times Magazine, March 16, 1975, p. 58.

[22]Robert L. Stern and Eugene Gressman, Supreme Court Practice, p. 342.

[23]Alexander M. Bickel, "The Caseload of the Supreme Court and What, If Anything, To Do About It," (Washington, D.C.: American Enterprise Institute for Public Policy Research, (1973), p. 36. Robert L. Stern and Eugene Gressman, Supreme Court Practice, p. 340. Glen Elsasser and Jack Fuller, "The Hidden Face of the Supreme Court," Chicago Tribune, April 23, 1978, Sect. 9, p. 44. Gerhard Casper and Richard A. Posner, "A Study of the Supreme Court's Caseload," in Sheldon Goldman and Austin Sarat, American Court Systems:

Readings in Judicial Process and Behavior (San Francisco: W. H. Freeman, 1978), pp. 144-154. See the chart, "How Cases Reach the Supreme Court," United States News and World Report, February 14, 1983, p. 39.

[24]Paul A. Freund, "Mr. Justice Brandeis," in Allison Dunham and Philip B. Kurland, Mr. Justice (Chicago: University of Chicago Press, Pheonix Books, 1964), p. 188.

[25]Alpheus Thomas Mason, Harlan Fiske Stone: Pillar of the Law (New York: Viking Press, 1956), p. 653.

[26]G. Edward White, The American Judicial Tradition. Profiles of Leading American Judges (New York: Oxford University Press, 1978), pp. 212-213. Chief Justice Charles Evans Hughes' "blacklist" - those petitions which he believed had no merit whatsoever - was rarely challenged. Joseph Tanenhaus, Marvin Schick, Mathew Muraskin, and Daniel Rose, "The Supreme Court's Certiorari Jurisdiction: Cue Theory," in Sheldon Goldman and Austin Sarat, American Court Systems: Readings in Judicial Process and Behavior (San Francisco: W. H. Freeman, 1978), p. 131.

[27]G. Edward White, The American Judicial Tradition, pp. 226-227.

[28]Theodore Voorhees, "The Resignation of Justice Holmes (Part 1)," 63 American Bar Association Journal, 263 (February, 1977) Theodore Voorhees, "The Resignation of Justice Holmes (Part 2)," 63 American Bar Association Journal, 426 (March, 1977).

[29]Theodore Voorhees, "The Resignation of Justice Holmes (Part 2)" Ibid., p. 426. In 1926 at age eighty-five, Holmes wrote Harold Laski, the British political theorist: "My work is over for the moment, but leisure comes never." Four years later, he writes Laski again: "There is a second breathing space after the second batch of certioraris has been returned . . ."

[30]Theodore Voorhees, "The Resignation of Justice Holmes (Part 1)," 63 American Bar Association Journal, 262 (February, 1977).

[31]Henry J. Abraham, The Judicial Process: An Introductory Analysis of the Courts of the United States, England, and France (3rd ed. New York: Oxford University Press, 1975), p. 183.

[32]Brown Transport Corp., petitioner v. Atcon, Inc. 58 L. Ed. 2d. 687 (1979).

[33]For a pointed piece buttressed by statistics, see Linda Greenhouse, "No Sign of Relief for an Overloaded Court," The New York Times, August 15, 1982, Section IV. See Chief Justice Warren Burger's court statistics as reported in the United States News and World Report, February 14, 1983, p. 39 and Linda Greenhouse's column "Burger's Opening Argument for a New Appellate Court." The New York Times, February 13, 1983, pp. 39-40.

[34]David W. Rohde and Harold J. Spaeth, Supreme Court Decision Making (San Francisco: W. H. Freeman Co., 1976), p. 131.

[35]David W. Rohde and Harold J. Spaeth, Supreme Court Decision Making, p. 33, note 28. Long before the controversy regarding the establishment of a National Court of Appeals but not as long ago as President Franklin Roosevelt's "packing" the Court scheme to help the "Nine Old Men," Arthur S. Miller discussed an over-burdened Court. See "A Note on the Criticism of Supreme Court Decisions," 10 Journal of Public Law, 139 (1961) reprinted in Miller's The Supreme Court Myth and Reality (Westport, Greenwood Press, 1978), pp. 89-103. A terse but excellent statement of "Proposals to Reduce the Supreme Court's Work," see Gerald Gunther, Constitutional Law: Cases and Materials (Mineola: The Foundation Press, 1975), pp. 75-80.

[36]David W. Rohde and Harold J. Spaeth, Supreme Court Decision Making, pp. 130-131.

[37]David W. Rohde and Harold J. Spaeth, Supreme Court Decision Making, p. 131. Lewis F. Powell, "Myths and Misconceptions About the Supreme Court," 61 American Bar Association Journal, 1345 (Nov. 1975). Alexander M. Bickel, "The Caseload of the Supreme Court and What, If Anything, To Do About It," (Washington, D.C.: American Enterprise Institute for Public Policy Research, 1973), p. 15. Erwin Griswold, former Solicitor General of the United States, says of Justice Douglas' statements: ". . . the vast leisure time we presently have . . ." and that ". . . we are vastly underworked . . ." says the following: "For anyone other than Justice Douglas this would seem to be hyperbole." Erwin N. Griswold, "Rationing Justice - the Supreme Court's Caseload and What the Court Does Not Do," 60 Cornell Law Review, 338, note 14 (1975). It was less Douglas's "egocentricity or perceived hypocrisy" that galled his colleagues as much as it was his "professional irresponsibility." It was bad enough not being a team player. Just as bad was his habit of disappearing to his favorite recreation area, Goose Prairie in the Northwest several weeks before the end of the term. James F. Simon, Independent Journey: The Life of William O. Douglas, (New York: Penguin Books, 1981), p. 432. On the Court's work hours see United States News and World Report. February 14, 1983, p. 38. See also John A. Jenkins, "A Candid Talk with Justice Blackmun," The New York Times Magazine, February 20, 1983, p. 61

that relates Blackmun's work schedule which is "lonely" for him
and "unfair" and "lonely" for his wife. David L. Kirp, Professor
of Public Policy at the University of California, Berkeley, has
deep misgivings about the Court going public. By taking to the
"hustings" the Court is beginning to resemble the political branches
something from which life tenure was expected to insulate them.
"The Justices Might Find A Gag's in Order," Wall Street Journal,
March 23, 1983, p. 30. The once courtly Court is changing. Some
of the Justices have not hesitated to utilize the opinions themselves for ad hominem or personal argument. There is less civility
and the discourse, on occasion, resembles politics and campaign
talk. Stephen Wermiel, "Low-Roading on the High Court," Wall
Street Journal, September 13, 1982 (editorial page).

[38]Richard L. Williams, "Justices Run 'Nine Little Law Firms'
at Supreme Court," (Part 2), Smithsonian, February, 1977, p. 91.

[39]Philip B. Kurland, "Jurisdiction of the United States
Supreme Court: Time for a Change," 59 Cornell Law Review 630
(April, 1974).

[40]Henry J. Abraham, The Judicial Process, pp. 197-198.

[41]Glen Elsasser and Jack Fuller, "The Hidden Face of the
Supreme Court," Chicago Tribune, April 23, 1978, Sect. 9, p. 47.

[42]Robert L. Stern and Eugene Gressman, Supreme Court Practice,
p. 341.

[43]Philip B. Kurland, "Jurisdiction of the United States
Supreme Court: Time for a Change," 59 Cornell Law Review, 628
(April, 1974). Chief Justice Burger - not overly friendly to
clerks - noted that there was a good deal of mythology about what
law clerks do. "And, of course, few law clerks do anything to
dispel that legend . . ." "Chief Justice Burger's Challenge to
Congress," United States News and World Report, February 14, 1983,
pp. 39-40.

[44]David W. Rohde and Harold J. Spaeth, Supreme Court Decision
Making, p. 123. Philip B. Kurland, "Jurisdiction of the United
States Supreme Court: Time for a Change," 631. Nina Totenberg,
"Behind the Marble, Beneath the Robes," The New York Times
Magazine, March 16, 1975, p. 58.

[45]Alexander M. Bickel, "The Caseload of the Supreme Court
and What, If Anything, To Do About It," p. 30.

[46]In addition to Professor Paul A. Freund, the other members
of the Study Group on the Caseload of the Supreme Court Committee
were: Alexander M. Bickel, Peter D. Ehrenhaff, Russell D. Niles,

Bernard G. Segal, Robert L. Stern, and Charles A. Wright. In 1972, the Congress established a commission representing all three branches of the Government to study the problems and make recommendations. This commission on Revision of the Federal Court Appellate System issued its report in June, 1975. Brown Transport Corp., petitioner v. Atcon, Inc., 58 L.Ed. 2d 687-688 (1979).

[47]David W. Rohde and Harold J. Spaeth, Supreme Court Decision Making, p. 130. Erwin N. Griswold, taking some of the Justices at their word that they are not "overworked," suggests a change in the proposed Freund Committee National Court of Appeals. See his "Rationing Justice - The Supreme Court's Caseload and What the Court Does Not Do," 60 Cornell Law Review, 335-354 (1975). For a short but concise discussion and cited literature see Edward L. Barrett, Jr., Constitutional Law: Cases and Materials (Fifth ed.: Mineola: The Foundation Press, 1977), pp. 50-58.

[48]Brown Transport Corp., petitioner v. Atcon, Inc., 58 L.Ed. 2d 687-695 (1979). The Chief Justice - "I have decided to be provocative on this issue" - continues to pressure Congress for relief. "Chief Justice Burger's Challenge to Congress," United States News and World Report, February 14, 1983. Despite his frustration in getting the attention of the nation and of Congress, Chief Justice Burger, not without humor, recalled that Chief Justice John Jay called for Appellate Courts in 1791 that were finally created in 1891. "I leave it to you," the Chief Justice said, "to decide how long we can wait." James Reston, "Crisis in the Courts?" The New York Times, November 21, 1982, Sect. 4.

[49]Ibid., 690. Justice Brennan's terse statement reads: "It seems appropriate, in light of footnote 7 of the Memorandum of the Chief Justice, to note my statement to the Commission, at 67 FRD, at 400, that Mr. Justice Brennan "remains completely unpersuaded, as he has repeatedly said, that there is any need for a new National Court." See also my article "The National Court of Appeals: Another Dissent," 40 U. Chi L. Rev 473 (1973).

[50]Nathan Lewin, "Avoiding the Supreme Court," The New York Times Magazine, October 17, 1976, pp. 90, 94.

[51]Nina Totenberg, "Behind the Marble, Beneath the Robes," p. 60. For a brief study of the Burger Court see William R. Thomas, The Burger Court and Civil Liberties (Brunswick: Kings Court Communications, 1976). An anonymous Justice admitted that in case selection he takes into account what its fate will be on the merits; and if to deny he will reject. "A decision may seem outrageously wrong to me, but if I thought the Court would affirm it, then I'd vote to deny. I'd much prefer bad law to remain the law . . . than to have it become the law of the land." Time, December 11, 1972, p. 73. See Saul Brenner, "The New Certiorari

Game," <u>Journal of Politics</u> 41 (1979) reprinted in S. Sidney Ulmer, <u>Courts, Law, and Judicial Processes</u>, p. 299.

[52]Nathan Lewin, "Avoiding the Supreme Court," p. 31. In his recent reaction against the Court's opinions, <u>Herbert v. Lando</u>, 60 L. Ed. 2d 115 (1979) and <u>Bell v. Wolfish</u> 60 L. Ed. 2d 447 (1979) as well as its judicial philosophy, its insensitivity to the poor and lack of protection for constitutional rights, Justice Marshall urged the lower court judges to read Wolfish narrowly and added: "All conceived reversals should be considered as no more than temporary interruptions" in the protection of individual rights. 65 <u>American Bar Association Journal</u>, 1037, (July, 1979).

[53]Nathan Lewin, "Avoiding the Supreme Court," p. 96.

[54]Richard L. Williams, "The Supreme Court of the United States: the Staff that Keeps it Operating," <u>Smithsonian</u>, January, 1977, p. 44.

[55]"How Reagan will Pick Judges is Unclear, but Philosophy Will Play an Important Role," <u>CQ Guide to Current American Government</u>, Fall, 1981 (Washington, 1981), pp. 124-126. James Reston, "Reagan and the Court," <u>New York Times</u>, March 13, 1983. When Potter Stewart resigned in July, 1981, President Reagan quickly appointed Sandra Day O'Connor of Arizona to fill the vacancy. As expected, she has tended to vote with the conservative bloc on federal/state issues. Yet she is also independent. See the early coverage of Justice O'Connor by Stephen Wermiel, "First Impressions of Justice Sandra Day O'Connor," <u>Wall Street Journal</u>, June 24, 1982; Linda Greenhouse, "High Court Version of the New Federalism?" <u>The New York Times</u>, June 6, 1982 and "The O'Connor Record Proves Surprising to Fans and Foes," <u>The New York Times</u>, July 11, 1982. Justice Harry Blackmun, very unusually, has gone public with his criticisms of Justice O'Connor, claiming she could easily succeed Burger as Chief Justice. Convinced she might have a political agenda, Blackmun says: "I have heard comments to the affect that everything she does looks as though she is running for President." John A. Jenkins, "A Candid Talk with Justice Blackmun," <u>The New York Times Magazine</u>, February 20, 1983, p. 57. One cannot help speculating what Justice Blackmun had in mind when he granted the <u>Times</u> such an unprecedented interview and the hour-long interview with Daniel Schorr, aired on public television, May 4, 1983.

VRJC LIBRARY

CHAPTER II

The "Politics" of "The Rule of Four"

Petitions for certiorari must win the votes of four members of the Court. This is called the "Rule of Four" and holds true even when only eight justices participate in the decision. For the petitioner this is a chancy and hazardous course and has, indeed, a very small success rate. Although four votes are necessary for a "grant" or a "note", a single Justice has the authority to bring up for full conference discussion any case or motion.[1] In politically sensitive cases, this becomes important and puts the Justice who has been asked to grant the writ under great public pressure. Nothing prevents a petitioner from shopping around and from convincing another judge. This recently occurred when Justices Byron White, first, and Thurgood Marshall second, each twice, refused relief to a New York Times reporter, M. A. Farber, who claimed he was being jailed unconstitutionally in violation of the free speech provision of the First Amendment.[2] On July 11, 1978, Justice White - as a result of Justice Brennan's disqualification - denied an application for stay involving a subpoena issued in the course of an ongoing criminal trial for murder and then added: "Of course, applicants are free to seek relief from another justice."[3] The New York Times and its reporter, Farber, then appealed to Justice Thurgood Marshall for an application, and the following day, July 12, he declined.[4] On August 1, Justice White denied a stay involving civil contempt against Farber and The New York Times,[5] and on August 4, Justice Marshall also denied a similar application.[6] When Justice William O. Douglas was savagely attacked for granting the Rosenberg's stay, Senator William Langer, Republican, North Dakota, offered him the following solace: "Douglas, they have thrown several buckets of shit over you. But by God, none of it stuck. And I am proud."[7]

Even if only eight Justices participate, it still takes four Justices to accept jurisdiction, but on rare occasions - as when six or seven Justices are eligible or available, the rule is sometimes but not invariably relaxed to permit the granting of certiorari on the vote of only three justices.[8] A justice can write a dissent on the refusal to hear a case as Douglas did when originally the conference denied certiorari to

Congressman Adam Clayton Powell of New York whom the House refused to seat. The Court not only took the case on the basis of his dissent but decided it 7 to 1 in favor of Powell.[9] Recently, Justices Marshall and Blackmun "dissented" from a denial of certiorari. In one case the issue involved the introduction of evidence at trial of a grand jury testimony and in the other a federal income tax case. These denials led Justice Stevens to write a blistering opinion condemning the practice. After quoting Justice Felix Frankfurter with approval that the "Rule of Four" is used as a matter of "sound judicial discretion," he went on to denounce the practive of writing "dissents" as "totally unnecessary;" the purist form of dicta;" devoid of "precedential significance at all;" "potentially misleading." Moreover, dissents do not carry the reasons denying certiorari and often exhibit "selected bits of information" which, in turn, "compromise the otherwise secret deliberations in our conferences" and weakens confidentiality so necessary "to the full and frank exchange of views during the decisional process."[10] "Some opinions dissenting from the denial of certiorari," note Robert L. Stern and Eugene Gressman, in Supreme Court Practice, "may reveal the majority's position on the merits."[11] In addition to the practice of a full written dissent from the denial of certiorari is the more prevalent practice of the short memorandum or paragraph. Justices Brennan, Stewart, and Marshall are particularly addicted to joining in numerous substantially identical dissenting opinions to denials of certiorari, and Justices Marshall and Brennan are frequently joined in issuing identical dissents in cases involving capital punishment.[12] On this point Stern and Gressman write:

> The repetition of identical language in opinion after opinion would seem to serve no useful purpose. Dissenting Justices whose strong convictions impel them to reiterate their position despite its continued rejection by the majority can do so merely by stating that "they dissent for the reasons stated" in prior cases, citing them.[13]

Commenting on this practice, Justice Stevens chides Justice Brennan for repeating this form of denial and adds for himself: "In the interest of conserving scarce law library space, I shall not repeat this explanation every time I cast such a vote."[14]

The Court itself is divided as to the meaning of

"The Rule of Four", even if it means, as in the case of denial, that the litigant has lost. On the one hand, Justice Robert Jackson's view was that it was a tacit agreement of a quorum that a case was not good enough and that the lower court decision should stand; on the other, it was Felix Frankfurter's view that it did not mean approval of a lower court decision at all but only that four justices did not think the matter ought to be adjudicated.[15] On balance it is probably correct to hold that the Justices deny certiorari to lower court cases because they are satisfied with the decision rendered. Denial could also mean that the Justices do not want to become involved in a political "hot potato" or that the Court is so divided on the issue that it is not prepared to take a stand.

In any event there is no rule of collective responsibility for decisions granting or denying certiorari. The group which controls the granting of certiorari, according to Glendon Schubert, has the power to define the questions among those raised by the petitioner and which the Court will accept for decision. It would not be unusual for the four Justices favoring review ultimately to find themselves in dissent after oral argument and judging the case on its merits.[16] Must a Justice denying review have an obligation to vote on the merits of the question which the Court has accepted for decision by its grant of certiorari? It would seem logical to suppose that when four Justices vote to hear a case that the other Justices are morally bound to judge it then on its merits. All the Justices accept this view except Justice Felix Frankfurter who claimed it violated his right to dissent and "not four not eight justices can require another to decide a case which he believes is not properly before the Court." The failure of a justice, he wrote, "to persuade his colleagues does not require him to yield to their views, if he has a deep conviction that the issue is sufficiently important."[17]

With this view, John Marshall Harlan, close to Frankfurter on many issues, disagreed because, on the one hand, to undo a grant of certiorari by voting, after the case had been heard to dismiss the writ as "improvidently granted", would hardly be fair to litigants who have spent time, effort, and money to have it decided on its merits; and on the other hand, it would emasculate "The Rule of Four" because any case warranting consideration by four should be disposed of.[18] In McCray the Court dismissed the writ of

23

certiorari as improvidently granted in a brief one
sentence note per curiam. Justices Brennan and Marshall
protested because one of the four Justices who had voted
to grant certiorari changed his mind after oral argument
and agreed to dismissal. "I hold the view", said
Justice Brennan, "that impermissible violence is done
the Rule of Four when a Justice who voted to deny the
petition for certiorari participates after oral argument in a dismissal . . ."[19] Justice John P. Stevens
did not participate in the petition but stated he would
vote to deny even if he had participated. The Court
should dismiss a writ once granted, he said, "when our
further study of the law discloses that there is no
need for an opinion of this Court on the question
raised by the petition."[20]

On more political grounds "The Rule of Four"
recently reaped a good measure of nasty publicity. The
secrecy of "the purple curtain"[21] was unveiled by Nina
Totenberg when she revealed a split over certiorari
petitions involving Watergate litigants John Mitchell,
H. R. (Bob) Haldeman, and John Ehrlichman. Neither
Chief Justice Warren Burger nor his "brothers" commented, but she alleged that the Chief Justice held up
a decision to announce a denial hoping to sway either
Justice Byron White's vote or that of John Paul Stevens.
Totenberg further claimed that Chief Justice Warren
Burger was politically manipulating the Court and its
decision-making process in behalf of conservative, even
reactionary, causes.[22] In the spring of 1979, another
leak occurred in the Court, and as a consequence, Chief
Justice Burger dismissed a typesetter from the court's
print shop after accusing him of leaking information to
a television correspondent. The Court also reduced
the number of hours during which reporters can use the
press room in the Supreme Court Building and ordered
that a police officer be stationed where he has a view
of the room.[23]

The Totenberg revelation was a deliberate leak
either by a justice or his clerk or anyone of a dozen
or more secretaries who have access to information
about the private conference. Totenberg said she put
the story together from several different sources. The
New York Times carried the story and then reported that
it had "confirmed" it "through other sources at the
Court."[24] Shooting from the hip, as it were, columnist
Max Lerner advocated "a press overview commission" like
the one Robert Hutchins urged years ago, forgetting
that it was a stillbirth on First Amendment libertarian

grounds. Law Professor Arthur Miller suggested making all "certs" public - a suggestion not taken very seriously. William Safire, columnist of The New York Times, called on Brennan, the most liberal member of the Court, to grant review and to throw out the government's case as "tainted". What is more important than guilt, he wrote, "is never as important as the upholding of due process."[25] Representing the Watergate defendants was Eugene Gressman, the distinguished co-author of Supreme Court Practice. Echoing Safire in part, he noted "that whatever the cause of the leak, the very fact that it occurred has impeded the even-handed administration of the Court's certiorari process to the detriment of the petitioners."[26] Eugene Gressman recalls five other leaks, and to his list Max Lerner, the journalist, adds two others.[27] Noteworthy, considering the length and controversial reputation of his Court, Chief Justice Earl Warren testified that there was never a leak during his time on the Court.[28] In his dissenting opinion in New York Times v. United States.[29] Chief Justice Warren Burger uses the issue of executive confidentiality to point up the necessity for confidentiality in the judicial process. The argument is based on inherent and not statutory power. "No statute gives this Court express power to establish and enforce the utmost security measures for the secrecy of our deliberations and records", he wrote. "Yet I have little doubt as to the inherent power of the Court to protect the confidentiality of its internal operations by whatever judicial measures may be required."

NOTES

CHAPTER II

[1]Lewis F. Powell, "What the Justices are Saying," 62 American Bar Association Journal, 1455 (November, 1976). Nina Totenberg, "Behind the Marble, Beneath the Robes," p. 58.

[2]The New York Times, August 6, 1978, p. 16.

[3]The New York Times v. Jascalevich, 58 L. Ed. 2d 11 (1979). If an application is denied by one Justice, it can be directed to another, although the Supreme Court Rule 50 (5) says that "such applications are not favored." Robert L. Stern and Eugene Gressman, Supreme Court Practice, p. 861. "A stay application that is acted upon by the Court requires the affirmative votes of a majority of the participating Justices if it is to be granted. If the Court is equally divided, the stay will be denied." Ibid., 862. Said Justice William O. Douglas: "Judges are not fungible; they cover the constitutional spectrum; and a particular Judge's emphasis may make a world of difference . . . Lawyers recognize this when they talk about "shopping for a judge." Arthur S. Miller, "The Supreme Court, the Adversary System, and the Flow of Information to the Justices," 61 Virginia Law Review, 1187 (1975) reprinted in Arthur S. Miller, The Supreme Court, Myth and Reality (Westport: Greenwood Press, 1978), p. 292.

[4]The New York Times v. Jascalevich, 58 L. Ed. 2d 14 (1979).

[5]The New York Times v. Jascalevich, 58 L. Ed. 2d 30 (1979).

[6]The New York Times v. Jascalevich, 58 L. Ed. 2d 44 (1979). The reporter (Farber) and Dr. Jascalevich (called Dr. X before his indictment) are chronicled and contrasted in Myron Farber, "Somebody Is Lying" The Story of Dr. X. (New York: Doubleday & Co., 1982).

[7]Rosenberg v. United States, 346 U.S. 273 (1953). Henry J. Abraham, The Judicial Process, p. 178. Robert L. Stern and Eugene Gressman, Supreme Court Practice, p. 866, note 97.

[8]John E. Nowak, Ronald D. Rotunda, and J. Nelson Young, Handbook of Constitutional Law (St. Paul: West Publishing Co., 1978), p. 40.

[9]Nina Totenberg, "Behind the Marble, Beneath the Robes," p. 58.

[10]Singleton v. Comm. of Internal Revenue, 58 L. Ed. 2d 337 (1978).

[11]Robert L. Stern and Eugene Gressman, Supreme Court Practice, p. 352.

[12]Justices Brennan and Marshall: "Adhering to our views that the death penalty is in all circumstances cruel and unusual punishment prohibited by the Eight and Fourteenth Amendments, . . . we would grant certiorari and vacate the death sentences in this case." Witt v. Florida, 54 L. Ed. 2d 294 (1977). Again Justices Brennan and Marshall: "Adhering to our views that the death penalty is in all circumstances cruel and unusual punishment prohibited by the Eight and Fourteenth Amendments . . . we would grant certiorari and vacate the death sentence in this case." Stephens v. Hopper 58 L. Ed. 2d 667 (1979). In dissenting from a denial of certiorari, Justices Marshall and Brennan, expatiate on the wrongness of capital punishment in Ford v. Arkansas, 74 L. Ed. 2d 519 (1983).

[13]Robert L. Stern and Eugene Gressman, Supreme Court Practice, p. 352.

[14]Liles v. Oregon, 425 U.S. 863. 964 (1976). The full force of Justice Steven's irritation is as follows: "The question we must first decide when acting on a petition for certiorari is whether we should set the case for full briefing and oral argument and thereafter decide the merits. Nothing in Mr. Justice Brennan's opinion dissenting from the denial of certiorari in this case persuades me that any purpose would be served by such argument. For there is no reason to believe that the majority of the Court which decided Miller v. California, 413 U.S. 15, 93 S. Ct. 2607, 37 L. Ed. 2d 419, is any less adamant than the minority. Accordingly, regardless of how I might vote on the merits after full argument, it would be pointless to grant certiorari in case after case of this character only to have Miller reaffirmed time after time. Since my dissenting Brethren have recognized the force of this reasoning in the past, I believe they also could properly vote to deny certiorari in this case without acting inconsistently with their principled views on the merits. In all events, until a valid reason for voting to grant one of these petitions is put forward, I shall continue to vote to deny. In the interest of conserving scarce law library space, I shall not repeat this explanation every time I cast such a vote." As for the increasing practice of writing dissents on a denial of certiorari, Justice Stevens called them "totally unnecessary" and examples of "the purest form of dicta." Singleton v. Comm. of Internal Revenue 58 E. Ed. 2d 337 (1978).

[15]Henry J. Abraham, The Judiciary, The Supreme Court in the Governmental Process (3rd ed.: Boston: Allyn and Bacon, 1973), p. 26. Daniel Berman, "Justice Frankfurter and the 'Rule of Four'," reprinted in Joel B. Grossman and Richard S. Wells, Constitutional Law and Judicial Policy Making, (New York: John Wiley & Sons, 1972), p. 152.

[16]Glendon A. Schubert, <u>Constitutional Politics. The Political Behavior of Supreme Court Justices and the Constitutional Policies That They Make</u> (New York: Holt, Rinehart & Winston, 1960), pp. 100, 101.

[17]<u>Ibid.</u>, p. 103.

[18]Daniel Berman, "Justice Frankfurter and the Rule of Four," reprinted in Joel B. Grossman and Richard S. Wells, <u>Constitutional Law and Judicial Policy Making</u>, p. 153.

[19]<u>Burrell v. McCray</u> 96 S. Ct. 2642 (1976).

[20]<u>Burrell v. McCray</u>, 96 S. Ct. 2641. See also 63 <u>American Bar Association Journal</u>, 104 (January, 1977).

[21]Glendon A. Schubert, <u>Constitutional Politics</u>, p. 115. Mary Ann Harrell's remark is not as firm today as formerly. She wrote: "In a capital full of classified matters, and full of leaks, the Court keeps private matters private." <u>Equal Justice Under Law. The Supreme Court in American Life</u> (rev. ed.: Washington, D.C.: The Foundation of the Federal Bar Association, 1975), p. 136. Harrell's remarks are more descriptive of the views of Chief Justice Morrison R. Waite. When Britton A. Hill, the attorney who argued against the Missouri Railroad, wrote Waite for an explanation regarding a story in a St. Louis newspaper that the Court had already reached a decision, the Justice tartly replied: "No such announcement has been made in the case" and "it would be highly improper for me to inform you, or anyone else whether a decision has yet been reached." Continuing, he said: "No one can deprecate more than I do the idea that the Court . . . can permit its secrets to be divulged. The importance of cases that come before us, as well as all the proprieties of judicial work, demand that, until our labors as a Court are ended, the secrets of the consultation room should be kept inviolate." C. Peter Magrath, <u>Morrison R. Waite the Triumph of Character</u> (New York: Macmillan, 1963), p. 277. Less open in recusing himself was Justice Brennan. Thomas G. Corcoran, an old Washingtonian brain-truster and New Dealer, approached Justice Brennan in the latter's chambers and urged the Justice to change his vote against the company in <u>El Paso Natural Gas Co. v. Southland Royalty</u>, 56 L. Ed. 2d 505 (1978). Critical of Brennan and citing this as an example of unnecessary secrecy on the Court. Alan B. Morrison inquired why a Justice who voted on the merits of a case one year had to recuse himself from considering the petition for a rehearing a year later? "Why wasn't Corcoran disciplined either by the Supreme Court or by other authorities for the obviously improper attempt to exercise behind-the-scenes influence?" "The Brethren: Focusing on the Wrong Secrecy," 66 <u>American Bar Association Journal</u> 566 (May, 1980). For leaks, near leaks, Court gossip and irrelevancies, a book to

be used with a good deal of caution is Bob Woodward and Scott Armstrong, The Brethren Inside the Supreme Court (New York, Avon, 1979). Comment on The Brethren has been heavy and perjorative. For one or two of the more scholarly pieces see Graham Hughes' review The New Republic, February 23, 1980, p. 30; Martin Shapiro, "Character Assassination by Attribution," Wall Street Journal, December 12, 1979, p. 24; John P. Frank, "The Supreme Court: The Muckrackers Return," 66 American Bar Association Journal, 160 (February, 1980). See Gerald T. Dunne, Hugo Black and the Judicial Revolution (New York: Simon & Schuster, 1977), pp. 243-244 for Court leaks disseminated by journalist Drew Pearson.

[22]Newsweek, May 9, 1977, p. 66. Muncie Star, April 28, 1977, p. 18. Harold J. Spaeth discusses this "leak," cites some of the "literature" dealing with it and adds: ". . . the 'leak' was an effort to embarrass the Court, not just the work of a gossipy clerk or Court employee." Supreme Court Policy Making. Explanation and Prediction (San Francisco: W. H. Freeman & Co., 1979), p. 141.

[23]The New York Times, May 19, 1979, p. 24. The New York Times, Sunday, June 3, 1979, Sect. 4, p. 19.

[24]Arthur John Keefe, "A Leak in the Supreme Court's Conference Muddies Justice," 64 American Bar Association Journal, 780 (May, 1978).

[25]Ibid., p. 781.

[26]Ibid., p. 782.

[27]Gressman's list is as follows: Dred Scott v. Sandford, 19 How. 393 (1857); Cummings v. Missouri, 4 Wall. 277 (1867); Ex parte Garland, 4 Wall. 333 (1867); the Legal Tender Cases, 12 Wall. 457 (1871); and Federal Power Commission v. Hope Natural Gas Company, 320 U.S. 591 (1944). Lerner's list comprises: Roe v. Wade 410 U.S. 113 (1973) and United States v. Nixon, 418 U.S. 683 (1974). 64 American Bar Association Journal, May, 1978, p. 781. The Court hoped in deciding Dred Scott that it would put an end to the sectional conflict but, instead, inflamed it and precipitated the Civil War. Wayne Andrews, Concise Dictionary of American History (New York: Charles Scribner's Sons, 1962), p. 304. The Court "suffered severely from self-inflicted wounds," and it "was many years before the Court . . . was able to retrieve its reputation." Charles Evans Hughes, The Supreme Court of the United States (New York: Columbia University Press, Garden City Publishing Co., 1936), pp. 50, 51. This "self-inflicted" wound was due, in part, to the leak in Dred Scott the information which was used in President James Buchanan's inaugural address delivered two days before the opinion was handed down. The new President made

reference to the forthcoming opinion asserting it would settle the territorial question. Republicans claimed Buchanan and the Court had conspired, and although unwarranted "by present day judicial standards the Court was guilty of highly unethical conduct in informing Buchanan in advance of its opinion so that he might use it for political purposes." Alfred H. Kelly & Winifred A. Harbison, The American Constitution: Its Origins and Development (New York: W. W. Norton & Co., 1948), p. 386.

[28]Earl Warren, The Memoirs of Earl Warren (New York: Doubleday & Co., 1977), p. 284. The Chief Justice went to extraordinary lengths to see that Brown v. Board of Education, 347 U.S. 483 (1954) was not leaked to the press. William O. Douglas, The Court Years 1939-1975, p. 115.

[29]The New York Times v. United States, 403 U.S. 713 (1971). The issue of leaks and confidentiality has tarnished the judicial integrity of the California Supreme Court with constitutional lawyers, Laurence Tribe and Raoul Berger (both of Harvard University Law School) differing. Tribe accents the Court's "confidentiality" and Berger, the Court's "accountability." 65 American Bar Association Journal, 1039 (July, 1979). See also Laurence H. Tribe, "Trying California's Judges on Television: Open Government or Judicial Intimidation?" 65 American Bar Association Journal, 1175-1179 (August, 1979). As was expected, an enterprising author has put the messy controversy into a hardcover book. Preble Stolz, Judging Judges: The Investigation of Rose Bird and the California Supreme Court (New York: Free Press, 1981). The Court issues its opinions and, in addition, conducts the oral conferences openly, but its conferences are protected from public scrutiny and disclosure under the Freedom of Information Act (1966). Harold Spaeth, Supreme Court Policy Making, p. 23.

JUSTICES AND CLERKS AND JUDICIAL DISQUALIFICATION

What role do the justices' clerks - currently numbering 32 - play in opinion writing? It is difficult to assess their influence. Chief Justice Burger already believes that the clerks have too much public exposure and are under too much pressure from the press and thus he refuses to supply the press with their names and backgrounds - a profound change from the attitude shown the first clerk who was hired in 1882 by Justice Gray mainly to be a servant and a barber.[1] On the critical side law clerks are viewed as legal Rasputins[2] with unfettered jurisdiction and unconfined power. Some critics would like to see them senatorially confirmed[3] - a move unlikely to materialize considering key congressional and White House aides are not confirmed. Professor Philip Kurland, himself a former law clerk, believes they play a detrimental role in "cert" memoranda in that they screen-out choices that the justices might never see. The main complaint of the Freund Report, he noted, was that somehow it threatened to reduce the powers of the choices of the Supreme Court and to turn it from its libertarian bent, but he admitted that he "should feel more sympathy for the criticism if it were based on fact . . . for the winnowing of the cases for judicial determination or petition for certiorari has already been delegated by most of the justices to their law clerks . . . who . . . rely for their judgments on certiorari one-page memoranda with a recommendation for grant or denial."[4] Kurland is supported by Professor Gerald Gunther who sees a correlation between the growing number of clerks and the growing length of opinions. In addition, the opinions are full of tangents and more confusing. Enthralled by their work the clerks "go off on some point of personal intellectual interest" that the Justices allow to slip by.[5]

Speaking of Justice Frank Murphy and Chief Justice Fred Vinson, Professor Kurland noted that neither had any great intellectual capacity, and, as a consequence, were absolutely dependent upon their law clerks for the production of their opinions.[6] After inquiring as to what was wrong with a Justice's assimilating the talents of his clerks, John Roche, in defense of Justice Murphy, adds: "However, I suggest that the law clerk gambit is

one best left unexplored, since who can tell how many
judicial reputations may be destroyed by candid revelation of what occurs in the chambers."[7] Before he was
appointed to the Court, ex-law clerk William Rehnquist
was extremely critical of the ideological bias of
clerks. Now, however, it is doubtful that Rehnquist,
the Justice, observed John Frank, "his own man if ever
there was one, still finds much cause for worry in this
quarter."[8] Professor Kurland has some support from
Chief Justice Harlan Stone's treatment of Justice
Murphy. The Chief Justice knew that he slighted
Murphy, and he often agreed to give him a "break", but
"in the end Murphy would be nosed out partly because
Stone disliked leaving a fine case to the rumination of
a law clerk."[9]

On the supporting side, it is difficult to believe
that a recent law school graduate, however brilliant,
could influence a seasoned Justice and alter his judgment during a one year appointment. In fact, despite
the high turnover of law clerks, it has been noted that
judicial viewpoints are consistent.[10] The clerks have
seen themselves as assistants but no more - certainly
not as a kitchen cabinet or as associates in opinion
writing.[11]

Clerks "circulate new energy".[12] They are trans-
mission belts,[13] a law school conduit, if you will,[14]
but while they give assistance, the ultimate choice of
rationale and analysis belongs to the Justice and is
not delegatable.[15] Each Justice uses his clerks to
best suit his style and his needs, but they are not
ghost writers in the White House sense. John Frank's
assessment in The Marble Palace is fairly typical: He
had one year as a clerk and participated in approximately 1000 decisions and concluded: "I had precisely
no influence on any of them."[16]

When should a Justice disqualify himself from
participating in a decision? On more than one occasion
the smooth functioning of the Court was shattered over
this issue. There is nothing in the Constitution about
disqualification of Justices. It is a matter left
entirely up to the responsibility of the Justice. There
is no statute on the subject, and the Court itself has
never ruled on it. There is no authority by which the
full Court has the power to exclude any one of the
Justices from participating or voting on a case.[17]
There is no mechanical rule, and each instance is
weighed and decided on its own merits. When a Justice

does disqualify himself, he seldom explains his reasons.[18] Some Justices are alert to conflicts of interest while others are more indulgent. Chief Justice Hughes followed a strict rule of not sitting in cases involving former clients or in which a former partner was counsel, and Justice Thurgood Marshall sat out some 31 out of 44 cases in the first five months of his appointment - cases which touched on his work as Solicitor General.[19] Justice Louis Brandeis, a model of personal rectitude, by contrast, continued to sit when former associates addressed the Court and in some instances heard cases involving corporations in which he had investments.[20] Nor did the great Chief Justice John Marshall disqualify himself in Marbury, inasmuch as it was Marshall, then serving as Secretary of State as well as Chief Justice, who had sealed but had not delivered Marbury's commission.[21] Justice Joseph Story, even making allowances for the times, transgressed judicial neutrality or fairness. He pressured the Treasury Department officials to secure large bank deposits in a Massachusetts branch bank of which he was President; he sat in cases involving the Bank of the United States while retaining his state bank presidency; he helped Daniel Webster draw up a reply to Jackson's veto of the National Bank Charter in 1832; and participated in the Charles River Bridge v. Warren Bridge (1837)[22] from which Harvard received an annual income from one of the litigants. This, despite Story's being on the Harvard faculty and a Fellow of the Corporation.[23] Taking a moderate position, Chief Justice Harlan Stone did not believe that it was necessary to abstain and disquality one's self in every instance and especially in cases of Justices who previously had been Attorney General and were connected in a "mere pro forma relationship . . . with cases in the Department of Justice."[24]

More recently, "recuse", the technical term of disqualification, touched Justices Hugo Black, William O. Douglas, and William Rehnquist, occasioning a good deal of Court bickering and public controversy. Voting with the majority in a five to four decision involving the United Mine Workers and the Jewel Ridge Coal Company, the latter asked for a rehearing because Justice Black's former law partner Crampton Harris was counsel for the labor union. Justice Black was accused of a conflict of interest. The Court was petitioned, but the hearing was denied. Customarily motions for a rehearing are denied without opinion, but in order to assuage Justice Jackson and Justice

Frankfurter, who believed that the basic fairness of the Court was at stake, Chief Justice Harlan Stone suggested a two sentence opinion denying a rehearing but inserting that the Court was not authorized and does not pass upon the propriety of a Justice not disqualifying himself. Justice Robert Jackson was willing to accept this statement but not Justice Black who threatened that "any opinion which discussed the subject at all would mean a declaration of war."[25]

In the midst of this quarrel in the Court, Chief Justice Harlan Stone died on April 22, 1946 and, as a consequence of a rumor that President H. S. Truman might appoint Justice Jackson as Chief Justice, a story surfaced that Justices Black and Douglas sometime earlier had informed President Franklin Roosevelt that they would resign if Justice Jackson were ever named Chief Justice.[26] Stung by Justice Black's "bullying" and his "declaration of war" and now by this public revelation of no confidence, by "this knifing", as Pusey calls it,[27] Justice Jackson, with Frankfurter concurring, challenged Black by issuing a statement of the Court's traditional handling of disqualification.[28] President Truman was aware of this feud and thus went outside the Court for a new Chief Justice, naming on June 7, 1946, Secretary of the Treasury, Fred M. Vinson, a crony and a politician of long political experience, whom the President believed was capable of unifying the Court and improving the public image.[29] He failed to do so.

Justice William Rehnquist participated in three cases in which he had been involved as Assistant Attorney General and in each case of a five to four vote cast the deciding vote for the Government. In Branzburg v. Hayes[30] (1972) the Court held that the First Amendment does not give journalists the right to refuse to disclose to grand juries the sources of confidential information, and in Laird v. Tatum[31] (1972) the Court held that the complainants lacked standing to protest military surveillance over civilians. In a case that grew out of "The Pentagon Papers", the Court ruled in Gravel v. United States[32] (1972) that Senator Gravel's legislative assistant, in connection with privately publishing "The Pentagon Papers", could be required to testify before a grand jury. The American Civil Liberties Union, counsel in the Laird case, petitioned for a rehearing and asked that Justice Rehnquist disqualify himself. Not only did Justice Rehnquist not recuse himself but published a 15-page memorandum indicating his reasons for not doing so.[33]

Justice Rehnquist cited several instances in which Court members, closely allied to an issue, nevertheless voted while on the Court. Thus, Justice Hugo Black who sponsored the Fair Labor Standards Act - called in the 1970 edition of the United States Code, the "Black-Connery Fair Labor Standards Act" - voted on the Court to uphold it; Justice Felix Frankfurter helped draft the Norris-LaGuardia anti-injunction act and wrote the Court's opinion in United States v. Hutchinson[34] (1962), interpreting the scope of the act and Attorney General Robert Jackson had decided an issue involving the deportation of an alien, and then as an Associate Justice, in McGrath v. Christensen[35] (1950) repudiated his former views.

After indicating other instances when Justices voted in cases in which they previously had participated in some way, Justice Rehnquist added:

> It would be not merely unusual, but extraordinary, if they had not at least given opinions as to constitutional issues in their previous legal career. Proof that a Justices' mind at the time he joined the Court was a complete tabla rasa in the area of constitutional adjudication would be evidence of lack of qualification, not lack of bias . . .[36]

An ABA code, dealing with conflict of interest, was adopted by the United States Judicial Conference in 1973, but the rule does not bind Justices of the Supreme Court, and it is unclear whether the Judicial Conference can sanction lower federal judges who disregard the rule.

Justice Rehnquist, at any rate, did not believe the rule (28 USC Section 455) covered him, for the Justice of the Supreme Court is different from federal lower court justices. "There is no way", he said, "of substituting Justices on this Court as one judge may be substituted for another in the district courts." Not only is there no higher Court of Appeals but the "disqualification of one Justice of this Court raises the possibility of an affirmance of the judgment below by an equally divided Court. The consequence attending such a result is, of course, that the principle of law presented by the case is left unsettled."[37]

37

The truth of Rehnquist's statement occurred in a case involving the <u>Aluminum Company of America</u>. Four Justices recused themselves because they previously had been involved in the issue. Because the Court lacked a quorum to decide the issue, Congress passed a special law giving jurisdiction of appeals in such cases (they would normally go to the Supreme Court) to the three senior judges of the circuit in which the case was tried.[38] In a case involving his old law firm that represented the <u>North American Company</u> in a dispute with the SEC, Chief Justice Harlan Stone disqualified himself and then recanted, explaining that when he announced his disqualification, he assumed a full Court which would not be true if he recused himself. He had, in a word, followed the rule of necessity.[39] In <u>Bailey v. Richardson</u> (1951) growing out of the time that he was Attorney General, Justice Tom Clark withdrew because of a conflict of interest and unavoidably caused a tie.[40] In 1970 Justice John Marshall Harlan removed himself from an important case involving oil shale mining rights, and the "niceties of judicial ethics dictated the cancellation of a Supreme Court hearing in mid-argument for Harlan's departure left but five Justices on the bench."[41] In <u>Public Utilities Commission v. Pollak</u>[42] (1952) where a majority found a deprivation of either the First or the Fifth Amendment because a city regulated bus company broadcast music and commercials, Justice Frankfurter was so irritated he recused himself saying:

> My feelings are so strongly engaged as a victim of the practice in controversy that I had better not participate in judicial judgment upon it. I am explicit as to the reasons for my non-participation in this case because I have for some time been of the view that it is desirable to state why one takes himself out of a case.

Despite the strong statement above by Frankfurter, he and Justice Louis D. Brandeis - the one dead 18 years and the other 42 years - hit the front page of <u>The New York Times</u> where, according to Danelski: "seldom does historical scholarship receive front-page coverage." What was disclosed Sunday, February 14, 1982 in the <u>Times</u> was that over a period of 23 years Justice Brandeis - then on the Court, paid Felix Frankfurter - then a Harvard Law School Professor - more than $50,000 to further the Justices' policy goals. This revelation was not entirely news - several books had hinted at

this arrangement and Bruce Allan Murphy who published
the Brandeis/Frankfurter Connection: The Secret Political Activities of Two Supreme Court Justices had previously revealed this relationship in 1980 in a Michigan
Law Review article. Within four days of the story the
Times said editorially that the association - however
high the motives - "was wrong" and "violated ethical
standards." Scholars and publicists have taken sides.
The debate continues and the literature is swelling.[43]

NOTES

CHAPTER III

[1]United States News and World Report, March 26, 1979, p. 37.
The writer does not know where the first clerk went to law school,
but in the 1965 Term, twelve of the nineteen clerks came from
Harvard, Yale, and the University of Pennsylvania law schools.
David W. Rohde and Harold J. Spaeth, Supreme Court Decision Making
(San Francisco: W. H. Freeman and Company, 1976), p. 69 note 40.

[2]William H. Rehnquist, "Who Writes Decisions in the Supreme
Court?" United States News and World Report, December 13, 1957,
pp. 74-75 reprinted in Robert Scigliano, The Courts: A Reader in
the Judicial Process (Boston: Little, Brown and Co., 1962), p. 167.

[3]James E. Clayton, The Making of Justice: The Supreme Court
in Action (New York: E. P. Dutton & Co., 1964), p. 63. Henry J.
Abraham, The Judicial Process: An Introductory Analysis of the
Courts of the United States, England, and France (3rd ed.: New
York: Oxford University Press, 1975), p. 238.

[4]Philip B. Kurland, "Jurisdiction of the United States
Supreme Court: Time for a Change," 59 Cornell Law Review, 627
(April, 1974).

[5]United States News and World Report, March 26, 1979, p. 33.
Since 1972 several of the Justices have been utilizing "cert-
pools" in which clerks from their chambers take turns writing a
"pool memo" on a batch of petitions which is then circulated among
them. This pool, of course, is in addition to a Justice's other
clerks they utilize. Mary Ann Harrell, Equal Justice Under Law,
p. 134. Robert L. Stern and Eugene Gressman, Supreme Court
Practice, p. 341. Said Justice Powell: "Each Justice is responsible for a personal judgment as to every petition, however much
he may delegate to his clerks." Doris Marie Provine, Case
Selection in the United States Supreme Court, p. 22.

[6]John P. Roche, "Mr. Justice Murphy," in Allison Dunham and
Philip B. Kurland, Mr. Justice (Chicago: University of Chicago
Press, Phoenix Books, 1964), p. 282. The idea of law clerk's
influence, said Justice Robert Jackson, gave rise to the waggish
statement that the Senate need not bother with the confirmation of
Justices "but ought to confirm the appointment of law clerks."
The Supreme Court in the American System of Government (Evanston:
Harper & Row, Harper Torchbooks, 1955), p. 20. One reason the
Court, although criticized, deserves its high reputation and is
likely to endure, says Justice Brandeis, is "it did its own work."
J. Harvie Wilkinson, Serving Justice: A Supreme Court's Clerk's
View (New York: Charterhouse, 1974), p. 15.

41

[7]John P. Roche, "Mr. Justice Murphy," in Allison Dunham and Philip B. Kurland, Mr. Justice, p. 284.

[8]J. Harvie Wilkinson, Serving Justice, p. ix. Justice Byron White was law clerk to Chief Justice Fred Vinson (1946-1947); John P. Stevens for Wiley Rutledge (1947-1948); and William Rehnquist for Robert Jackson (1952-1953). Richard L. Williams, "Justices Run 'Nine Little Law Firms' at Supreme Court," (Part 2), Smithsonian, February, 1977, p. 86.

[9]Alpheus Thomas Mason, Harlan Fiske Stone: Pillar of the Law (New York: Viking Press, 1956), p. 793. For a discussion of Justice Murphy and his clerks see J. Woodford Howard Jr., Mr. Justice Murphy: A Political Biography (Princeton: Princeton University Press, 1968), pp. 242, 267, 459, 474. Chief Justice Stone stated a "principle" and asked his clerks to support it with relevant citations - whether in dissent of or in majority of even his own opinions. Wrote William O. Douglas: "Frankfurter and I labeled Stone's passion for citing his own opinions as "Stone's disease." The Court Years 1939-1975, p. 171.

[10]J. Harvie Wilkinson, Serving Justice, p. 58.

[11]Glen Elsasser and Jack Fuller, "The Hidden Face of the Supreme Court," Chicago Tribune, April 23, 1978, Sect. 9, p. 19.

[12]Nina Totenberg, "Conflict at the Court," Washington Magazine, February, 1974 reprinted in Annual Editions, Readings in American Government '77 - '78 (The Dushkin Publishing Group, Inc., Sluice Dock, Guilford Ct., 1977), p. 146.

[13]J. Harvie Wilkinson, Serving Justice, p. 66.

[14]Alexander M. Bickel, "The Law Clerks," in Aaron Wildavsky and Nelson W. Polsby, American Governmental Institutions (Chicago: Rand McNally, 1968), p. 305.

[15]Lewis F. Powell, "What the Justices are Saying," 62 American Bar Association Journal, 1454 (November, 1976).

[16]John P. Frank, Marble Palace: The Supreme Court in American Life (New York: Knopf, 1958), p. 118. Fred Rodell believes the clerks are influential. They gave Chief Justice Warren ". . . the precedents, the library references, the footnotes when he wanted them." "It is the Earl Warren Court," The New York Times Magazine, March 13, 1966, p. 93.

[17]Glendon A. Schubert, Constitutional Politics, p. 148. Alpheus Thomas Mason, "When Should a Judge Disqualify Himself?" in Robert Scigliano, The Courts, A Reader in the Judicial Process

(Boston: Little, Brown, 1962), p. 367. See Arthur S. Miller, "Public Confidence in the Judiciary," 35 Law and Contemporary Problems (Durham: Duke University School of Law, Winter, 1970) reprinted in Arthur S. Miller, The Supreme Court Myth and Reality (Westport: Greenwood Press, 1978), pp. 326-329. Stephen Wermiel, "Financial Interests on the Supreme Court," The Wall Street Journal, August 4, 1981 (ed. page).

[18]James E. Clayton, The Making of Justice: The Supreme Court in Action (New York: E. P. Dutton, 1964), p. 160.

[19]Henry J. Abraham, The Judicial Process, p. 200 note 100.

[20]Merlo J. Pusey, Charles Evans Hughes (New York: Macmillan Co., 1952), II, pp. 679-680.

[21]Marbury v. Madison 1 Cr. 137 (1802). Robert F. Cushman, Cases in Constitutional Law (4th ed.: Englewood Cliffs: Prentice-Hall, 1975), p. 10. John E. Nowak, Ronald D. Rotunda, and J. Nelson Young, Handbook of Constitutional Law (St. Paul: West Publishing Co., 1978), p. 2.

[22]11 Pet. 420 (1837).

[23]G. Edward White, The American Judicial Tradition. Profiles of Leading American Judges (New York: Oxford University Press, 1976), p. 41.

[24]Alpheus Thomas Mason, Harlan Fiske Stone, p. 703.

[25]Ibid., p. 644. James E. Clayton, The Making of Justice, p. 160. J. Woodford Howard, Jr., Mr. Justice Murphy, pp. 391-394. One of the impeachment charges against Justice William O. Douglas that the special House Judiciary subcommittee dealt with was an alleged conflict of interest with the magazine Avant Garde and also Eros. Justice Douglas failed to disqualify himself from those court cases that involved the publisher, Ginzburg. The Supreme Court: Justice and the Law (Washington, D.C. Congressional Quarterly, September, 1977), p. 42. See Gerald T. Dunne, Hugo Black and the Judicial Revolution, p. 199, 234-240 for a discussion. Dunne says Black emerged the winner and, moreover, could not lose for even if he had disqualified himself a tie division on the Court would have affirmed the lower court decision. Ibid., p. 246. William O. Douglas, The Court Years 1939-1975 adds little that is new to the controversy, pp. 29-30.

[26]G. Edward White, The American Judicial Tradition, p. 234. The two sides on the Black-Jackson dispute are ably set forth in Eugene C. Gerhardt, America's Advocate: Robert H. Jackson (Indianapolis: Bobbs-Merrill, 1958) and John P. Frank, Mr. Justice

Black (New York: Knopf, 1949). Justice Black's son writes: "It was a plain lie. Dad had said no such thing. We never knew who had been responsible for the misinformation that was passed to Justice Jackson." Hugo Black, Jr., My Father: A Rememberance (New York: Random House, 1975), p. 191. Gerald T. Dunne, Hugo Black and the Judicial Revolution, pp. 225-226, 241-242.

[27]Merlo J. Pusey, Charles Evans Hughes, II, p. 802.

[28]Glendon A. Schubert, Constitutional Politics, p. 148. G. Edward White, The American Judicial Tradition, pp. 234, 238, 405.

[29]Leon Friedman and Fred I. Israel, The Justices of the United States Supreme Court 1789-1969 Their Lives and Major Opinions (New York: Chelsea House and R. R. Bowker Co., 1969), IV, p. 2641. It was former Chief Justice Charles Evans Hughes and Justice Roberts that advocated Fred Vinson. Both told Truman: "You don't need to look any further. The Chief Justice is administrator. He's administrator of the Courts; he's got to be a man who can make the Court get along together, and everybody likes. You've got the man in your cabinet - Fred Vinson." See Alpheus Thomas Mason, "The Chief Justice of the United States: Primus inter Pares," 17 Journal of Public Law, 56 (1968).

[30]Branzburg v. Ohio, 408 U.S. 554 (1972).

[31]Laird v. Tatum, 408 U.S. 1 (1972).

[32]Gravel v. United States, 408 U.S. 606 (1972).

[33]Laird v. Tatum, 409 U.S. 824 (1972). Federal laws of 1976 and 1979 - but not 1977 and 1978 - stopped or reduced previously authorized cost of living increases for federal judges. The Court claimed this violated the Constitutional prohibition against diminishing judges' pay. This dispute, of course, seemed to put the Court in violation of conflict of interest sentiments. Rehnquist's opinion leans heavily on the Rule of Necessity." United Stated v. Will, 66 L. Ed. 2d 392 (1980).

[34]United States v. Hutchinson, 369 U.S. 599 (1962).

[35]McGrath v. Kristensen, 340 U.S. 162 (1950).

[36]Laird v. Tatum, 409 U.S. 824 (1972).

[37]Ibid.

[38]Robert L. Stern and Eugene Gressman, Supreme Court Practice, p. 2, 3 notes 7, 8.

[39]Alpheus Thomas Mason, Harlan Fiske Stone, p. 703.

[40]Henry. J. Abraham, The Judicial Process, pp. 199-200.

[43]Ibid., p. 178.

[42]Public Utilities Commission v. Pollack, 343 U.S. 467 (1952).

[43]David J. Danelski's quotation is found in his excellent essay-review of Murphy's book, The Brandeis/Frankfurter Connection: The Secret Political Activities of Two Supreme Court Justices (New York: Oxford University Press, 1982) printed in the Harvard Law Review, vol. 96, November, 1982, p. 312. The New York Times quotation is from the issue of February 18, 1982 at A 22, col. 1. For a sampling of other comments and reviews see the two news reports in The New York Times for February 14 and 21, 1982 written by David M. Margolich; the review by Arthur Schlesinger, Jr. The New York Times Book Review, March 21, 1982, p. 5; the review by Joseph Barbato, The Chronicle of Higher Education, April 7, 1982, p. 25; Nelson W. Polsby, Commentary, May, 1982 p. 96; Gary L. McDowell, The American Political Science Review, vol. 76, No. 4, December, 1982, p. 913; and, finally, Michael W. Steinberg, 68 American Bar Association Journal, 716 (June, 1982).

CHAPTER IV

RAIDING THE COURT

What depresses a Chief Justice is the constant
attempt of most Presidents to raid the Court of its
members for some special assignment. These are not
always taken unwillingly, for some Justices are politically ambitious.[1] Charles Evans Hughes, as Associate
Justice, was drafted to run against President Woodrow
Wilson in 1916. This criticism surfaced in 1930 when
President Herbert Hoover nominated Hughes as Chief
Justice. Justice Oliver W. Holmes supported Hughes
saying: "I don't so much mind Hughes having left the
bench and coming back. Lots of our judges have had the
presidential bee . . ."[2] David Davis "was regarded as
a candidate (1872) of politicians both Republican and
Democratic and "the presidency burned feverishly in
Chase's mind, and he would take any road that led
there."[3] When the Court is being decimated and is in
a state of flux, it poses problems for the Chief Justice,
especially in his assignment role, in voting on cases,
and in preserving the Court's image of equal justice
under law.

President Grover Cleveland offered Chief Justice
Melville Fuller the post of Secretary of State which he
declined saying that to do so, no matter how eminent
the position, would detract "from the dignity and weight
of the tribunal."[4] When he accepted an appointment to
the Court, said Chief Justice Waite, he felt it was his
duty "not to make it a stepping-stone to something
else . . ."[5] In another instance President William
McKinley asked Chief Justice Fuller to serve on the
Spanish-American Peace Commission, but he refused
saying: "It is far wiser that the Chief Justice should
not participate in public affairs," a refusal he forgot
and then regretted when in 1897 with Justice David
Brewer, he accepted an appointment as an arbitrator in
the boundary dispute between Venezuela and British
Guiana.[6]

By contrast, Chief Justice William H. Taft luxu-
riated in offering political advice, solicited or not.
He accepted assignments which not only took him away
from the Court - such as his confidential mission to
the League of Nations of which the United States was
not a member - but which also required him to lobby

47

Congress, the American Bar Association, and newspaper
editors. Chief Justice William H. Taft ". . . actively
intervened, as has no Chief Justice before or since, to
promote the candidacies of his friends and to block
those of others."[7] He even wrote for the commercial
press but not with the same ease that Justice William
O. Douglas later did.[8] In an article Chief Justice
Taft wrote for _Collier's_ magazine, he later wondered
about the propriety of his action. "I shrink from the
publicity that you are giving to the article," he wrote
the editor. "It is not of sufficient importance, and
I cannot help doubting the propriety of my having given
you the interview."[9]

Of all the Presidents, it seems, Franklin D.
Roosevelt had no hesitation in depleting the Court for
political ends and, in doing so, caused no little
anguish to Chief Justice Harlan Stone.[10] Lamented the
Chief Justice: "I am doing," he said:

> all I can by way of precept and example
> to counteract the unfortunate tendency of
> federal judges, including those of my own
> court to dilute their judicial influence
> and efficiency by engaging in extra-
> judicial activities.[11]

Despite Attorney General Francis Biddle's report that
the Court was short handed because Justice Byrnes had
been absent for ten months working with the President,
Roosevelt kept waving the Attorney General aside
impatiently saying, "let's keep it open for Jimmy; they
can get along."[12] In conflict with his own intention
of naming younger men to the Court, President Roosevelt
astounded Attorney General Biddle with the suggestion
that the President would appoint "some old boy for two
or three years who could agree to retire when he had
reached seventy, so that Jimmy could be brought back."[13]

President Woodrow Wilson had wanted Justice Louis
Brandeis, during World War I, to head some war-related
agency, and Chief Justice Edward D. White objected.
When Brandeis offered to resign from the Court, Wilson
replied: "Not on your life. On that bench you are more
important to the country than you could possibly be
elsewhere. It was too difficult to get you there to
take a chance of losing you through a temporary
appointment."[14] President Wilson had not forgotten
that he had nominated Brandeis to the Court January 28,
but it was not until June 1, 1916 that, over very

strong opposition, he was confirmed by the Senate.[15]

Several other extra judicial assignments marred
the smooth functioning of the Stone Court, each one in
some way war related. It was bad enough that Chief
Justice Harlan Stone learned it from the press, but he
was strongly aroused when Justice Frank Murphy entered
military service. The Chief Justice raised the question
of holding down two jobs and getting two salaries when
the Constitution prohibited this, but apparently Murphy
had violated no statute in accepting an army commission.[16] Stone's outburst did not provide much of a
reason, and at any event Murphy's induction impressed
Americans as being a very patriotic thing to do. It is
more likely that Chief Justice Stone, who had little
confidence in Justice Frank Murphy to begin with, was
irked by this show of independence and also by the fact
that the Stone Court was disintegrating.[17] Chief
Justice Stone was the titular leader among equals and
had to contend with strong personalities.[18] He
attempted to keep the Court out of the press except on
opinion day but was not successful.

If Justice Murphy's caper irritated Chief Justice
Stone, Justice Owen Robert's decision to head a Congressional Commission on Pearl Harbor, December, 1941
(it did not conclude its formal report until July,
1946) and Justice Robert Jackson's participation as the
American Prosecutor at the Nuremberg War Crimes trials
unsettled him.[19] The Chief Justice could not understand why the President could not select someone from
the 130 million other Americans who were not on the
Court. Justice Jackson's participation at Nuremberg
was distasteful to Stone on several counts: he dis-
approved in principle of non-judicial work, he objected
to the trials on legal and political grounds, and he
knew of the consequences of Jackson's absence to an
overburdened Court. There were a number of 4 to 4
cases that were in limbo, and in the meantime, the
Chief Justice felt that Justice Jackson was not doing
his share of opinion writing. In addition to Justice
Stone's comment that Jackson's absence caused the work
of the Court to slow down, it is believed that Jackson's
overwork and fatigue at Nuremberg was partly responsible
for his public attack on Justice Hugo Black over Fred
Vinson's appointment as Chief Justice.[20] For Justice
Jackson, though, the Nuremberg experience was ". . .
the most important and enduring and constructive work
of his life."[21]

49

It does not come as a surprise to learn that even after his appointment Chief Justice Fred Vinson continued to discuss politics with his old friend, President Harry Truman. They enjoyed one another's company and late in the evening conversed on the telephone. Chief Justice Vinson was President Truman's first choice as his successor, but the Chief Justice declined to run. On one occasion, President Truman wanted Chief Justice Vinson to go to Moscow and to talk to Joseph Stalin, but Secretary of State George Marshall vetoed the idea.[22] Despite the fact that the Chief Justice failed to unify the Court, he did reduce its tensions. He lacked the intellectual power to surmount the deep-seated intellectual differences, and, notwithstanding his enormous political experience, he could not manage the Court's conference in any sophisticated way.[23]

Allowances made for the political sorties of a Chief Justice do not necessarily cover Associate Justices. It could be that Justice Abe Fortas did not come out of the Congress where he might have had natural allies, but his too close association with President Lyndon Johnson was one of the indiscretions that led to his rejection by the Senate as Chief Justice when Earl Warren resigned and was a factor which ultimately led to his resignation.[24] The first Justice ever to resign on political grounds, Justice Abe Fortas had participated in diplomatic conferences and advised the President on simmering social conditions. Neither Justice Fortas nor President Johnson "could see . . . wrong in their continuing relationship." The Senate did.[25]

Easily the most celebrated and also the most political - considering the kind of legal entanglements that could generate from the appointment - was Chief Justice Earl Warren's chairmanship of the President's Commission on the Assassination of President John F. Kennedy. Initially, Chief Justice Warren was dead set against serving. When President Lyndon Johnson called and asked him to come to the White House, the Chief Justice sent a personal note ahead telling the President that he opposed serving on constitutional grounds and would refuse if asked. Then the President, saying that the country truly needed him to get through the bloody tragedy of the assassination and that Warren's personal integrity was a key element in unearthing facts convinced him that the conclusions would be credible. The country was confronted with threatening divisons and suspicions, and, as Johnson reports it, ". . . you

50

are the only man who can handle the matter, you won't say 'no', will you?"[26] As he recalls that interview with the President, Chief Justice Warren responded: "Mr. President, in spite of my feelings about the matter, if you consider it of that importance, of course, I will do it."[27] Chief Justice Warren spent ten months on the Commission, "the unhappiest year of my life" and ". . . a traumatic experience . . ." in which he divided his long day between the Court and the Commission.[28] The contrast in political experience between Justice Jackson at Nuremberg and Chief Justice Warren on the Commission has to be explained by the political atmosphere and the international outlook of each man, for each was engaged in an equally distasteful work, the former unmasking and judging perpetrators of genocide, and the latter, investigating the brutal assassination of a youthful President.

According to the Truman _Memoirs_, the President's offer to send Chief Justice Fred Vinson to Moscow was declined, but Vinson said that if the President made it a presidential request, "I shall have a clear duty to comply." President Truman then told Chief Justice Vinson that he regretted it, but in the interest of the country and world peace, "I am compelled to request you to go."[29] One cannot but wonder how vigorous the doctrine of separation of powers is when a President can "request" the Chief Justice of the United States to leave his post.[30]

NOTES

CHAPTER IV

[1]Alepheus Thomas Mason, <u>Harlan Fiske Stone</u>, p. 269. In
general see Henry J. Abraham, <u>Justices and Presidents: A Political
History of Appointments to the Supreme Court</u> (New York: Oxford
University Press, 1974).

[2]Alpheus Thomas Mason, <u>Harlan Fiske Stone</u>, p. 281, 704.

[3]Herbert Eaton, <u>Presidential Timber: A History of Nominating
Conventions, 1860-1960</u> (Glencoe: The Free Press, 1964), p. 3. See
the appendix of Bruce Allen Murphy, <u>op cit</u>, which recounts the
political activities of the Supreme Court Justices from 1789 to
1916. When Justice Lewis Powell came to the Court, he thought that
specialized fields would operate nicely. He later changed his
mind saying: "My brothers gently rejected my proposal, reminding
me that I was being paid to render personal judgments. If there
were a central staff of specialists it would often be their judgments that ended up in the United States reports. The wisdom of
their view, although initially accepted with some chagrin, is now
self-evident to me." "What the Justices are Saying," 62 <u>American
Bar Association Journal</u>, 1454 (November, 1976).

[4]Leon Friedman and Fred L. Israel, <u>The Justices of the United
States Supreme Court 1789-1969 Their Lives and Major Opinions</u>, II,
p. 1492-1493.

[5]<u>Ibid</u>., 1249. President Harry S. Truman had no qualms about
raiding the Court and suggested that Chief Justice Fred Vinson become a presidential candidate. The President citing the Hughes
precedent in which Charles Evans Hughes had resigned from the
Court in order to run against Woodrow Wilson, added: ". . . that
in my opinion there would be nothing wrong in (Vinson) becoming a
candidate." Harry S. Truman, <u>Memoirs</u> (New York: Doubleday, 1952),
II, p. 490.

[6]<u>Ibid</u>., pp. 1492-1493. Willard L. King, <u>Melville Fuller:
Chief Justice of the United States 1888-1910</u> (New York: Macmillan,
1950), p. 249.

[7]G. Edward White, <u>The American Judicial Tradition</u>, p. 179.
See Walter F. Murphy, "In His Own Image: Mr. Chief Justice Taft
and Supreme Court Appointments," in Philip B. Kurland, <u>The Supreme
Court and the Constitution: Essays in Constitutional Law from the
Supreme Court Review</u> (Chicago: University of Chicago Press,
(Phoenix Books, 1965), pp. 122-157. For Chief Justice Taft's
numerous forays in off-the-bench political activity, see Alpheus T.

Mason, William Howard Taft: Chief Justice (New York: Simon and Schuster, 1965), pp. 138-156.

[8]The Supreme Court: Justice and the Law (2nd ed. Washington, D.C.: Congressional Quarterly, 1977), p. 42.

[9]Leon Friedman and Fred L. Israel, The Justices of the United States Supreme Court 1789-1969 Their Lives and Major Opinions, III, p. 2110. Justice William O. Douglas did not "shrink" from the publicity his books and articles produced - especially his book Points of Rebellion (1970) that presented the thesis that violence could be justified. Perhaps only revolutionary overthrow of the establishment could save the country. His writings appeared in the Evergreen Review which also contained nudes. The Supreme Court: Justice and Law (2nd ed. Washington, D.C.: Congressional Quarterly, 1977), p. 42. One of the charges of Congressman Jerry Ford (later, of course President Ford) that led to the proposed impeachment of Justice Douglas grew out of Points of Rebellion. James F. Simon, Independent Journey: The Life of William O. Douglas (New York: Penguin Books, 1981), pp. 391-411.

[10]Leon Friedman and Fred L. Israel, The Justices of the United States Supreme Court 1789-1969 Their Lives and Major Opinions, III, p. 2111. President Herbert Hoover in his inaugural address called for reform of the judicial system and the enforcement system and to this end proposed a commission on law observance. At first, Chief Justice Taft acquiesced on Hoover raiding the Court of, say, Justice Van Devanter or even Brandeis, but when Hoover suggested Justice Harlan Fiske Stone, the Chief Justice opposed it. The Court supported Taft. "With the Court on his side, Taft refused to call the Justices back to conference to discuss Hoover's plea." Alpheus Thomas Mason, William Howard Taft: Chief Justice, (New York: Simon and Schuster, 1965), pp. 153-155.

[11]Alpheus Thomas Mason, Harlan Fiske Stone, pp. 712-713. President Franklin Roosevelt also attempted to get Justice William O. Douglas to serve as coordinator for National Defense purchases but Douglas refused. The Court Years 1939-1975, pp. 267-268.

[12]Joel B. Grossman, "The Politics of Judicial Selection," in Joel B. Grossman and Richard S. Wells, Constitutional Law and Judicial Policy Making (New York: John Wiley & Sons, 1972), p. 202.

[13]Francis Biddle, "An Inside View of Appointing Supreme Court Justices," in Joel B. Grossman and Richard S. Wells, Constitutional Law and Judicial Policy Making (New York: John Wiley & Sons, 1972), p. 207.

[14]Alpheus Thomas Mason, Brandeis: A Free Man's Life (New York: Viking Press, 1946), p. 526. President Lyndon Johnson had

no qualms about raiding the Supreme Court to make a high political
appointment and, as a consequence, in diluting the liberal "bloc."
Justice Arthur Goldberg accepted an appointment as the United
States Ambassador to the United Nations and wrote the President:
"I shall not, Mr. President, conceal the pain with which I leave
the Court after three years of service. It has been the richest
and most satisfying period of my career." Stephen L. Wasby,
Continuity and Change: From the Warren Court to the Burger Court
(Pacific Palisades: Goodyear Publishing Co., 1976), p. 27 note 9.
John Kenneth Galbraith in A Life in Our Times: Memoirs takes credit
for convincing President Johnson to ask Justice Goldberg to switch
to the United Nations as the American Ambassador. Now contrite,
Galbraith claims the Court lost a good liberal. "I did little for
liberalism that morning." Reviewing the Memoirs, James Fallow
says that Galbraith inflates his own importance and that it is
more likely that President Johnson wanted the seat vacant in order
to appoint Abe Fortas his long time friend. The New York Times
Book Review, May 3, 1981, pp. 24-25.

[15]Alpheus Thomas Mason, Brandeis: A Free Man's Life, pp. 465-
508. By contrast, former Senator Harold Burton was confirmed without the customary hearings. Charles Van Doren and Robert McHenry,
Webster's American Biographies (Springfield: G & C Merriam, 1975),
p. 158. George Sutherland, who succeeded Justice John A. Clarke,
"was confirmed unanimously by the Senate, an endorsement not even
Taft himself had received." G. Edward White, American Judicial
Tradition, p. 185. George Sutherland, like Burton, was a former
Senator. He served for 13 years between 1904 and 1917. He was
also President of the American Bar Association 1916-1917. Justice
Sandra Day O'Connor, unlike Burton and Sutherland, was not a
member of "the Club" - the citadel as William White called it in
Citadel: The Story of the United States Senate (1957). She was
confirmed 99-0 and Senator Max Baucus, (D) Montana who supported
her nomination in the Judiciary Committee happened to be absent
from the Senate during the vote. "Senate Confirms O'Connor as
Supreme Court Justice," Congressional Quarterly, September 26,
1981, p. 1831. What started out as a debate on her confirmation
turned into a love gathering. The Senate takes its confirmation
power seriously. It has refused to confirm 26 out of 136 Supreme
Court Justices submitted for its approval. Henry J. Abraham,
Justices and Presidents, p. 31. For a chart covering the nominee,
President, date of nomination, and date of Senate action, see
The Supreme Court: Justice and the Law (2nd ed., Washington, D.C.:
Congressional Quarterly, 1977), p. 27.

[16]Alpheus Thomas Mason, Harlan Fiske Stone, p. 708. For a
discussion of Murphy's military service and the bickering with
Chief Justice Stone that it caused, see J. Woodford Howard, Jr.,
Mr. Justice Murphy: A Political Biography (Princeton: Princeton
University Press, 1968), pp. 273-278.

[17]John P. Frank, <u>Marble Palace: The Supreme Court in American Life</u> (New York: Knopf, 1958), p. 80.

[18]G. Edward White, <u>The American Judicial Tradition</u>, p. 227.

[19]<u>Ibid.</u>, p. 236.

[20]John P. Frank, <u>Marble Palace</u>, p. 258. See Gerald T. Dunne, <u>Hugo Black and the Judicial Revolution</u>, p. 225-226. According to Justice Douglas, he plus Stone, Black and Murphy thought the Nuremberg Trials were unconstitutional by American standards. <u>The Court Years 1939-1975</u>, p. 28.

[21]G. Edward White, <u>The American Judicial Tradition</u>, p. 248.

[22]Harry S. Truman, <u>Memoirs: Years of Trial and Hope</u> (Garden City: Doubleday & Company, 1956), II, p. 217. Leon Friedman and Fred L. Israel, <u>The Justices of the United States Supreme Court 1789-1969 Their Lives and Major Opinions</u>, IV, p. 2648. President Woodrow Wilson, like Justice Brandeis, deemed it improper to ask a Justice to the White House on a matter necessarily political. Alpheus Thomas Mason, <u>Brandeis: A Free Man's Life</u>, p. 522. Chief Justice Earl Warren dropped all political friendships, and as he reported to Anthony Lewis: ". . . I felt it necessary to divorce myself from every political activity of every kind and to try to act in a non-partisan way as it is possible for a human being to do. I tried also to eliminate every influence from personal contacts that could be brought to bear upon me." Anthony Lewis, "A Talk with Warren on Crime, the Court, the Country," <u>The New York Times Magazine</u>, October 19, 1969, p. 129. Chief Justice Warren underscored this view later in his <u>Memoirs</u> saying, also, that while he attended protocol dinners, he and Mrs. Warren rarely accepted invitations to private homes "because that called for reciprocation." Earl Warren, <u>The Memoirs of Earl Warren</u> (New York: Doubleday, 1977), p. 345. It seems like a prudent practice to read judicial memoirs as material falling in the "suspect classification." Disingenuously or innocently because of a faulty memory or whatever, memoirs tend to be disjointed, incomplete, fragmentary, and often deficient in matters from jurists although trained in "legal reasoning." It could be that Justices are even more political than supposed from what we know of the selection process. From their memoirs, autobiographies, and biographies, it appears not infrequently that the Senate is more concerned with their political and social views than strictly legal questions. See the excellent essay-review of "Earl Warren. Master of the Revels" by Philip B. Kurland of G. Edward White's <u>Earl Warren: A Public Life</u> (1982) 96 <u>Harvard Law Review</u>, pp. 331-339 (November, 1982). Similarly, a safe guide to Justice William O. Douglas's memoirs, <u>The Court Years 1939-1975</u> is James E. Simon, <u>Independent Journey: The Life of William O. Douglas</u> (New York: Penguin Books, 1981).

But President Roosevelt's Attorney General, Francis Biddle, almost surely declined a seat on the Court because he did not want to be "cut-off from the world and out of things." Francis Biddle, "An Inside View of Appointing Supreme Court Justices," in Joel B. Grossman and Richard S. Wells, Constitutional Law and Judicial Policy Making, p. 208. Some Justices have found it necessary to "scorn delights and live laborious days . . ." Thus, "Brandeis and Cardozo were almost as retired as hermits and Chief Justice Hughes withdrew from all social engagements except one night a week . . ." Robert H. Jackson, "Advocacy Before the Court: Suggestions for Effective Case Presentation," 37 American Bar Association Journal, 863 (November, 1951). Two short sympathetic essays pointing up the spartan lives of Brandeis and Cardozo can be found in Sidney H. Asch, The Supreme Court and Its Great Justices (New York: Arco Publishing Co., 1971), pp. 103-116, 143-159.

[23]John P. Frank, Marble Palace, pp. 85, 86. Leon Friedman and Fred L. Israel, The Justices of the United States Supreme Court 1789-1969 Their Lives and Major Opinions, IV, p. 2641. The Court contains leadership roles, especially task leader and social leader, in addition to the role as Chief Justice. Thus, on the Taft Court, Chief Justice Taft was the social leader, and Van Devanter, the task leader. Chief Justice Hughes was both a social and task leader, while Chief Justice Harlan Stone was not only a poor task leader but was challenged by Justice Hugo Black. Sheldon Goldman and Thomas P. Jahnige, The Federal Courts as a Political System (New York: Harper & Row, 1971), pp. 180-181. Harlan Fiske Stone was almost sixty-nine when he succeeded Chief Justice Charles Evans Hughes. Although Stone is listed among the "Twelve Greats" - see Albert P. Blaustein and Roy M. Mersky, The First One Hundred Justices, Statistical Studies on the Supreme Court of the United States (Hamden: Archon Books, 1978), p. 37 - nevertheless he was "clearly more comfortable in being a member of the team than in leading it . . . (and) his reluctance to crack down and his aversion to do battle with warring factions contributed to a marked divisiveness on the Court during his Chief Justiceship . . ." Henry J. Abraham, Justices and Presidents, pp. 217-218. By contrast, John Marshall's great influence was due, in part, to his social leadership. ". . . he was at the head of the family as much as he was chief of a court." Samuel Krislov, The Supreme Court in the Political Process, (New York: Macmillan, 1965), p. 56. Justice William O. Douglas contrasts the conference under Chief Justice Hughes and Chief Justice Stone. Stone, he concludes, believed in freedom of speech for everyone including himself, continually postponed conferences so that the Court was "almost in continuous conference." The Court Years 1939-1975. p. 222.

[24]For the political and media aspects of the events that led to the Fortas and the Senate vote, see Samuel Sheffer, On and Off the Floor, Thirty Years as a Correspondent on Capitol Hill (New York: Newsweek Books, 1980), pp. 79-94. Also on Fortas'

resignation, see The Supreme Court: Justice and the Law (2nd ed. Washington, D.C.: Congressional Quarterly, 1977), pp. 35-36. For a complete discussion see, Robert Shogan, A Question of Judgment: The Fortas Case and the Struggle for the Supreme Court (Indianapolis: Bobbs-Merrill, 1972).

[25]Henry J. Abraham, Justices and Presidents, p. 263. The Supreme Court: Justice and the Law, p. 162. Robert Shogan, A Question of Judgment, p. 113. President Lyndon Johnson first appointed Justice Abe Fortas because he believed him "the most experienced, compassionate, articulate and intelligent lawyer I knew" and nominated him Chief Justice subsequently because "his progressive philosophy, his love of country, his frank views always spoken from the heart, and his service to the Presidency . . ." and the charges of his enemies that Fortas violated the principle of the separation of branches by "acting as a counselor to the President from time to time while serving on the Courts" is a flimsy argument, in fact, "a straw man, pure and simple." The real reason, wrote President Johnson, was that Republicans and Southern conservatives "were horrified at the thought of a continuation of the philosophy of the Warren Court." Lyndon Baines Johnson, The Vantage Point: Perspectives of the Presidency 1963-1969 (New York: Holt, Rinehart and Winston, 1971), pp. 545-546. During the hearings on his nomination as Chief Justice, Fortas made the same appeal to history as President Johnson did. See Walter F. Murphy, Elements of Judicial Strategy (Chicago: University of Chicago Press, 1964), pp. 147-150. Professor Arthur S. Miller writes: "Left unstated by the former Justice is how past conduct of others which may in itself have gone beyond propriety can justify present activity;" moreover, as a former law professor, "Fortas would hardly have accepted in the classroom such an argument as he put forth in his attempt to justify his continuing to be personal counselor to the President after becoming a Justice." See Arthur S. Miller, "Public Confidence in the Judiciary," Law and Contemporary Problems (Durham: Duke University School of Law, Winter, 1970), reprinted in Arthur S. Miller, The Supreme Court Myth and Reality (Westport:Greenwood Press, 1978), p. 328 plus note 88. See also, Note, "Must a Supreme Court Justice Refuse to Answer Questions?" 78 Yale Law Journal, 696-712 (1969) for an excellent discussion of the Senate hearings. The account, while in general sympat'.etic to Fortas, is ultimately critical of him because, as a res ilt of a position he took in which he would not comment on cases 'even when there (was) no danger of prejudging a future case" and thus by ". . . declining to defend the Court, he missed an opportunity to educate the people, and perhaps even the Senate." Ibid., 712. Little did Fortas realize that two stories, both silly, that circulated in Washington would harm him. Once he was in an elevator with distinguished lawyers, judges, and administrators and it stopped. While everyone else waited to be rescued, Fortas opened a panel, pulled a lever and the elevator started. With mock innocence he said to his fellow passengers:

"It's really quite simple, for an insider." In 1965 Fortas listed his business for an edition of Who's Who in the South West as "presidential adviser, c/o the White House, 1600 Pennsylvania Avenue, Washington, D.C." See the tribute to Justice Fortas made before a special session of the Court by the Solicitor General Lee. Miscellaneous Proceedings, 74 L. Ed. iii (March 29, 1983).

[26]Lyndon Baines Johnson, The Vantage Point, p. 27.

[27]Anthony Lewis, "A Talk with Warren on Crime, the Court, the Country," The New York Times Magazine, October 19, 1969, pp. 133-134.

[28]Ibid., 133. Leon Friedman and Fred L. Israel, The Justices of the United States Supreme Court 1789-1969 Their Lives and Major Opinions, II, p. 2723. On substantive and procedurel grounds, Justice Felix Frankfurter in retirement was very critical of Chief Justice Warren and quite derogatory of the Warren Commission. Bernard Schwartz, "Felix Frankfurter and Earl Warren: A Study of a Deteriorating Relationship" in Philip B. Kurland and Gerhard Casper (eds.), The Supreme Court Review, 1980 (Chicago: Chicago University Press, 1981), pp. 132-133.

[29]Harry S. Truman, Memoirs: Years of Trial and Hope, II, p. 214.

[30]A unique role the Court played in the political process grew out of the Hayes-Tilden Election of 1876. Congress created an Election Commission of fifteen members composed of five representatives, five Senators, and five Supreme Court Justices. This bipartisan Commission contained seven Republicans and seven Democrats. The fifth Justice selected, presumably, was an independent. He was David Davis. But Davis was named to the Senate in 1877 and was replaced by Joseph Bradley who voted with the Republicans on every major Commission vote. Hayes received the disputed electoral votes and won the election. There is some evidence that Justice Bradley voted under pressure although he always denied it. He said politics did not influence him. "I know that it is difficult for men of the world to believe this, but I know it, and that is enough for me." G. Edward White, The American Judicial Tradition, p. 93. The Democrats always believed that pure partisanship deprived them of the presidency. See John A. Garraty, The New Commonwealth 1877-1890 (New York: Harper & Row, Harper Torchbooks, 1968), pp. 259-260.

CHAPTER V

THE CONFERENCE AND THE POLITICS OF ASSIGNMENT

The Justices are called to conference by a buzzer that rings in the several chambers five minutes before the conference hour. The conference room is oak-paneled and contains bookcases from the floor to the ceiling with lower and Supreme Court opinions. There is one portrait of the fourth and greatest Chief Justice, John Marshall. Each Justices' chair is different and bears a name plate. Justices are seated according to seniority. Serving the Justices is the main law library of some 210,000 books and a staff of 14. Each Justice has an agenda of the cases to be discussed and, in addition, a movable cart containing all the materials he might need in discussion.

There are no clerks, stenographers, pages, or even a tape recorder present. There is absolute secrecy and confidentiality. If it is necessary to get material from outside the conference chamber or to answer the door, the most recently appointed Justice acts as "doorkeeper". Whatever the length of time, Justice O'Connor will be the "doorkeeper" until a new Justice is appointed. Justice Tom Clark was the Junior Justice for five years, and he was fond of relating that he "was the highest paid doorkeeper in the world." So rarely is the conference disturbed that Chief Justice Earl Warren reports that during the sixteen years he was Chief Justice, the conference telephone never rang once.[1]

The Chief Justice opens the discussion by indicating the judicial history of the case and the precise question before the Justices. Although the Chief Justice is the first among equals, he has a triple advantage: he opens the issue and in so doing sets the tone of the discussion and the direction in which it could lead; votes last, exercising a "swing vote" in five to four decisions; and if in the majority, he assigns the opinion to himself if it is a "landmark" case, or if it is not to someone else. If the decision is considered a "landmark" case, or one of great public importance, the Chief Justice is expected to write it himself and thus throw the weight of the Court behind it. The Chief Justice might recognize the political consequences of external politics and select a Justice whose views will carry great weight.[2]

If the Chief Justice is in the minority, he does not assign the opinion but rather the senior Justice in the majority does. Chief Justice Burger's use of the assignment power recently encountered criticism that involved an abortion decision and Justice Douglas. The latter claimed that the Chief Justice had sided with the minority in conference but voted with the majority expressly to preserve the prerogative of assigning the opinion. This was done when Burger was accused of voting "open" when some people believed that he had already made up his mind.[3]

Dissents, of course, are not assigned. Majority opinion assignments are not made at the conference but formally in writing several days later.[4] The leadership role here is evident, for the Chief Justice, in assigning an opinion, can indicate that he favors one approach rather than another. He may make the decision more or less acceptable to the public, help retain a narrow majority, and win over a dissenter to the majority.[5] Perhaps the classic example of a Chief Justice's dominating opinion assignment was John Marshall's voting with the majority, although in opposition, so that he could write the Court's opinion.[6] During the 34 years Marshall served on the Court, he wrote 519 of the 1,006 opinions handed down.[7] This record is not likely to be equaled ever or even approximated, but during the sixteen years Earl Warren was Chief Justice, he assigned 80% of the opinions. As Edward G. White put it: "The Chief Justice presides, to be sure, over arguments, conferences, and other functions, but he also listens and defers and yields."[8]

"I often had in mind the special fitness of a Justice for writing in the particular case", said Chief Justice Charles E. Hughes, although he was careful to avoid specialization.[9] Hughes had told Merlo Pusey, who later wrote a distinguished biography of the Chief Justice, that he felt, "every Justice should have a chance to demonstrate through the writeup of opinions the wide range of his reasoning powers and not be kept before the public as an extremist or specialist working in one particular groove."[10] While Chief Justices William H. Taft and Harlan F. Stone did not use their assignment powers to influence a unanimity, it appears that Chief Justice Hughes did.[11] It is not uncommon for a Chief Justice, in the interests of a smooth functioning Court, to retain the dullest and most

boring cases. This was true of Chief Justices Melville
Fuller, William H. Taft, Charles E. Hughes, and Earl
Warren.[12] Chief Justice Earl Warren also assigned to
himself those cases that promised to be condemned most
vigorously.[13] Warren was willing to reach, however,
". . . beyond the academic critics of his methods to
the public beneficiaries of his acts."[14]

The Chief Justice might have policy goals but he
must be viewed as impartial in the assignment of opinions. "I do not believe," said Chief Justice Warren,
"that if assigning opinions wasn't done with regard to
fairness,

> it could well lead to great disruption
> in the Court. During all the years I was
> there . . . I did try very hard to see
> that we had an equal work load . . .
> Everybody, regardless of the length of
> time they were on the Court, had a fair
> opportunity to write important cases."[15]

The Chief Justice also testified that in all the years
he was on the Court, he "never had any of the Justices
urge me to give them opinions to write."[16]

Almost every Chief Justice has assigned opinions
for "political reasons". Thus, Chief Justice Harlan
Stone assigned the Japanese Relocation case, Korematsu,
to Justice Hugo Black, considered a liberal; Chief
Justice Earl Warren assigned Justice Tom Clark, a
southerner and practicing Protestant, Schempp, which
involved the separation of Church and State; and Chief
Justice Charles E. Hughes assigned conservative Justice
George Sutherland the first Scottsboro case, Powell,
upholding Negro rights to counsel.[17] Chief Justice
Hughes also on occasion assigned "liberal" opinions to
"conservatives" and vice versa "in order to disabuse
the public of the notion that the Court was divided
along simple liberal and conservative lines."[18] For
reasons of strategy Thurgood Marshall, a black, was
assigned McDonald v. Santa Fe Transportation Co.[19]
(1976) in which he held that Title VII of the 1964
Civil Rights Act prohibited employers from discrimi-
nating against whites on the basis of their race in
and to the same extent it prohibits racial discrimination against blacks.

In an unusually delicate instance, Chief Justice
Harlan Stone, had assigned Smith v. Allwright[20] (1944),

a case invalidating racist southern primaries, to
Justice Felix Frankfurter. Justice Robert Jackson
sent the Chief Justice a memorandum, calling it unwise
and urged him to withdraw it, which the Chief Justice
did. Justice Frankfurter, wrote Jackson, united in a
rare degree factors which unhappily excite prejudice
for,

> In the first place, he is a Jew. In the
> second place, he is from New England,
> the seat of the abolition movement. In
> the third place, he has not been thought
> of as a person particularly sympathetic
> with the Democratic party in the past.

Justice Robert Jackson convinced Chief Justice Harlan
Stone that the assignment to Justice Frankfurter "may
grate on Southern sensibilities," and thus the Chief
Justice reassigned the opinion to Justice Stanley Reed,
a white Protestant and Kentucky Democrat before his
appointment to the Court.[21]

There are limits to the internal politics of
assignment inasmuch as the Chief Justice "must bear in
mind the law specialities of the Justices, their rela-
tive ability to handle and write opinions under a
heavy load of cases, and the realities of external
politics as well."[22] Justice Van Devanter developed
"pen paralysis" and could scarcely write five opinions
yearly. He came to the conference very well prepared
with his ideas developed and his arguments marshalled,
"thus possibly securing votes before any writing
began."[23] Chief Justice Harlan Stone had very little
confidence in Justice Frank Murphy, he practically
never assigned him anything of importance.[24] It was
only when the Chief Justice was in the minority and
Justice Hugo Black, the senior Justice assigned the
opinion, did Justice Murphy get an important case.[25]
It is always a delicate matter when a Justice has difficulty "in pulling his weight" because of age, infir-
mity, psychology or some other reasons. Short of
impeachment (which is unlikely since the "disability"
would not be constitutionally covered) and a mandatory
retirement age (which the Congress will not pass),
each Court deals with these problems as best as it can.
Thus, in December, 1974, Justice Douglas suffered a
stroke which not only curtailed his work but apparently
the work of the entire Court. The number of opinions
written decreased, and eleven cases were set for
reargument (only one the previous term). "These

statistics indicate that the Court may have deferred
decisions in cases in which Douglas' vote might be
decisive."[26]

   In assigning an opinion, the Chief Justice selects
a Justice who is closest to the dissenters so that the
opinion will be accepted.[27]   The Chief Justice must
select someone who will choose the ground most likely
to hold the majority together.[28]   An opinion is the
work of a single judge but it is also an institutional
product; it is a "desperately negotiated document."[29]
Justice Louis Brandeis, for example, was assigned Erie
Railroad Company v. Tomkins[30] (1938) which overruled
Swift v. Tyson[31] (1842) and took in too much ground.
Instead of sticking to the statutory question, he slid
into the constitutional one.   Chief Justice Hughes complained, but because Brandeis did not budge, Hughes
agreed to go along "for the sake of harmony."[32]   In
consensus building the Chief Justice knows that one
Justice is more suitable than another Justice for purposes of "public relations".[33]   The assignment power
can be instrumental in determining the value of a case
as a precedent, of making a decision as acceptable as
possible to the public, of holding the Chief Justice's
majority together when the conference vote is close
and of persuading dissenting associates to join the
Court's opinion.[34]

CHAPTER V

¹Earl Warren, The Memoirs of Earl Warren, p. 383. Richard
L. Williams, "Justices Run 'Nine Little Law Firms' at Supreme
Court," (Part 2), Smithsonian, February, 1977, p. 88. See also
Chief Justice Earl Warren's rare television interview with Dr.
Abraham Sachar, Chancellor of Brandeis University. This was tele-
cast on May 3, 1972. The transcript is printed in Sheldon Goldman
and Austin Sarat, American Court Systems: Readings in Judicial
Process and Behavior, (San Francisco: W. H. Freeman, 1978),
pp. 520-521. Chief Justice William H. Taft once remarked that
the ". . . experiences of a Chief Justice are like those of an
impresario with his company of artists." Elliot Slotnick, "Who
Speaks For the Court? The View From the States," 26 Emory Law
Journal, pp. 115-116 (1977). Using the same idea, Justice Felix
Frankfurter observed: "In Court and in Conference (Hughes) struck
the pitch, as it were, for the orchestra." "The Administrative
Side of Chief Justice Hughes," 63 Harvard Law Review 3 (November,
1949). For an excellent short but meaty discussion of the Chief
Justice see Alpheus Thomas Mason, "The Chief Justice of the United
States Primus Inter Pares," 17 Journal of Public Law, 20-60 (1968).

²G. Edward White, The American Judicial Tradition, p. 204.
Danelski is quoted as follows: "But what the opinions contain
depend largely upon their authors, and they are selected by the
Chief Justice. Thus when the Chief Justice decided who shall
speak for the Court, he makes a decision which may be crucial not
only in the judicial process but in the political process as well."
Elliot E. Slotnick, "Who Speaks For the Court? The View From the
States," 26 Emory Law Journal, 108 (1977). Magrath makes somewhat
the same point by noting that while the Justices are equal in
Conference, "reputation and public recognition are acquired by
writing opinions." C. P. Magrath, Morrison R. Waite: The Triumph
of Character (New York: Macmillan, 1963), p. 262. John Frank put
the Chief Justices' power this way: "The man who selects the issues
to be talked about very frequently dominates the end results."
Marble Palace, p. 75. The Chief Justice's retention of "big cases"
is generally accepted by his associates. "In fact, they expect
him to speak for the Court in those cases so that he may lend the
prestige of his office to Court's pronouncement." David J. Danelski, "The Influence of the Chief Justice in the Decisional Process," in Walter F. Murphy and C. Herman Pritchett, Courts, Judges,
and Politics: An Introduction to the Judicial Process (2nd ed. New
York: Random House, 1974), 530. William O. Douglas, The Court
Years 1939-1975, p. 37. See Walter F. Murphy, Elements of Judicial
Strategy (Chicago: University of Chicago Press, 1964), pp. 84-85.
Richard E. Johnson, "Some Comparative Statistics on Chief Justice
Opinion Writing" 26 Western Political Quarterly, 457 (1973).

The most "apparent finding is the willingness of the Chief Justices
to write opinions when such cases arise." Chief Justice Taft wrote
the majority opinion in thirty-four percent of the important cases,
Chief Justice Hughes, twenty-nine percent and Chief Justice Stone,
seventeen percent. David W. Rohde, "Policy Goals, Strategic
Choice and Majority Opinions Assignments in the United States
Supreme Court," 16 Midwest Journal of Political Science, 656 (1972).
Chief Justice Waite consistently assigned the most important cases
to the ablest man on the Court and in seventy-two cases decided
between 1874 and 1881 of constitutional significance, Waite "voted
against the majority in only six, thereby giving him the right of
assigning the other sixty-six." C. Peter Magrath, Morrison R.
Waite: The Triumph of Character, p. 263. Chief Justice Warren
assigned the largest number of significant cases to himself in
addition to assigning over seventy-five percent of all opinions
during the period that Professor Ulmer studies. Interestingly,
too, Chief Justice Warren chose to write at a six percent rate in
5-4 cases - a vote less than half that of any other Justice leading Professor Ulmer to suppose that Chief Justice Warren was willing to "let Frankfurter do it" and thus "avoided calling attention
to situations in which his ability to lead the Court appeared
marginal." S. Sidney Ulmer, "The Use of Power in the Supreme
Court. The Opinion Assingments of Earl Warren, 1953-1960," 19
Journal of Public Law 67 (1970). See S. Sidney Ulmer, "Leadership
and Group Structure," in S. Sidney Ulmer, Courts, Law, and Judicial
Processes for the leadership advantage the Chief Justice has in the
Court's conference. In the desegregation case, Brown v. Board of
Education 347 U.S. 483 (1954) ". . . Warren exploited his oppor-
tunity to the full." pp. 374, 379.

[3]Glen Elsasser and Jack Fuller, "The Hidden Face of the
Supreme Court," Chicago Tribune, April 23, 1978, Sect. 9, p. 50.
Harry Shriman, Letter, 62 American Bar Association Journal, 700
(June, 1976). Surprisingly, Elliot E. Slotnick who studied opinion
assignment on the state supreme court level found that ". . . in
over twenty-five percent of the states, the Chief Justice always
assigns majority opinions, whether he is in the majority or not."
"Who Speaks For the Court? The View From the States," 26 Emory Law
Journal, 111 (1977). Although the opinion assignment, according to
Sidney Ulmer, "Analysis of Behavior Patterns in the United States
Supreme Court," 22 Journal of Politics 629, 642 (1960) "is clearly
the most important duty of the Chief Justice in relation to his
associates" in the United States Supreme Court, it is interesting
to note that state opinion assignments vary with the greatest
majority of the courts (48.9%) using one or another rotation system.
Elliot Slotnick, "Who Speaks for the Court? View From the States,"
26 Emory Law Journal, 111 (1977). The arguments advanced for the
rotation practice include: (1) the ease with which clerks and court
administrators can operate it; (2) it removes the potential for
unfair treatment; (3) saves the Chief Justice time in not agonizing
over assignments; and (4) guards against the development of narrow

experts. <u>Ibid</u>. Justice William O. Douglas calls attention to the charge that Chief Justice Warren Burger voted "open" in order to control assignments. <u>The Court Years 1939-1975</u>, p. 232.

[4]David W. Rohde and Harold J. Spaeth, <u>Supreme Court Decision Making</u> (San Francisco: W. H. Freeman and Company, 1976), p. 189. Henry J. Abraham, <u>Freedom and the Court: Civil Rights and Liberties in the United States</u> (3rd ed.: New York: Oxford University Press, 1977), p. 194. William J. Brennan, Jr., "Inside View of the High Court," in Leonard W. Levy, <u>The Supreme Court Under Earl Warren</u> (New York: New York Times Co., Quadrangle Books, 1972), p. 43. See Nina Totenberg, "Behind the Marble, Beneath the Robes," <u>The New York Times Magazine</u>, March 16, 1975 that discusses C. J. W. Burger. The assignment is never or rarely made at the Conference but is made rather several days later. William J. Brennan, Jr., "Inside View of the High Court," p. 41. Writes Slotnick: "The Chief Justice is generally pictured as going into seclusion after the judicial conference and re-emerging at the next conference with opinion assignments in hand. At most he is said to have conferred with a trusted law clerk or colleague on the bench." The assignment view "is seen as a very private and independent series of decisions . . ." Elliot Slotnick, "Who Speaks For the Court? The View From the States," 26 <u>Emory Law Journal</u>, 116, (1977). The grounds for assignment, said Justice Felix Frankfurter, may not always be obvious to the outsider. "Indeed, they are not always so to the members of the Court; the reasons normally remain within the breast of the Chief Justice. But these involve, if the duty is wisely discharged, perhaps the most delicate judgment demanded of the Chief Justice." "The Administrative Side of Chief Justice Hughes," 63 <u>Harvard Law Review</u> 4 (November, 1949). One of the greatest of the Chief Justices - perhaps second to Marshall - namely, Charles Evans Hughes, claimed that if the inner workings of the Court were widely known and understood, popular respect of the judiciary would be vindicated. See Walter F. Murphy, <u>Elements of Judicial Strategy</u>, (Chicago: University of Chicago Press, 1965), p. viii.

[5]Sheldon Goldman and Thomas Jahnige, <u>The Federal Courts As A Political System</u>, p. 181. See the following exchange: David N. Atkinson and Dale A. Neuman, "Toward a Cost Theory of Judicial Alignments: The Case of the Truman Bloc," 13 <u>Midwest Journal of Political Science</u>, 271-283 (1969) which deals with the "cost" of concurring and dissenting opinions and David W. Rohde, Comments on "A Cost Theory of Judicial Alignments," 14 <u>Midwest Journal of Political Science</u>, 331-336 (1970) as well as David N. Atkinson and Dale A. Neuman "On Understanding the Limits of the Cost Theory: A Reply," <u>Ibid</u>., 337-338 (1970). Among the reasons an opinion is assigned to a particular Justice in marginal cases are the following possibilities: (1) the Justice occupies a pivotal position and the assignment is a "payoff" or reward to hold the majority together; (2) the Justice is closest in view to the assigning

Justice; (3) the Justice ". . . has some unusual attraction" for
one or more members of the opposition group; and (4) the Justice
". . . represents what is common to the bloc to which he belongs
rather than some extreme position." "Every Chief Justice," says
Justice Douglas, "when assigning opinions, has an eye to public
relations and to history - and naturally so." William O. Douglas,
The Court Years 1939-1975, p. 34.

[6]Sheldon Goldman and Thomas Jahnige, The Federal Courts As
a Political System, p. 10.

[7]W. Melville Jones, Chief Justice John Marshall: A Reap-
praisal (Ithaca: Cornell University Press, 1956), p. xv.
G. Edward White, The American Judicial Tradition, p. 12. In
Marshall's first five years as Chief Justice, he wrote the opinion
in every case in which he participated and in the next seven years
he wrote the opinion of the Court in 130 cases, assigning a total
of only thirty cases to his colleagues. Walter F. Murphy,
Elements of Judicial Strategy, p. 85. See "Marshall's Method and
Technique in Deciding Cases," in Charles Grove Haines, The Role
of the Supreme Court in American Government and Politics 1789-1835
(Berkeley and Los Angeles: University of California Press, 1944),
pp. 630-639. From Marshall's time on the Court, 1801-1835, there
were 1,244 opinions issued and the Chief Justice wrote 508 or 41%
of them. In his thirty-four years there were only seventy dissenting opinions with Marshall writing six of them. Albert P. Blaustein and Roy M. Mersky, The First One Hundred Justices, p. 97.
Chief Justice Waite was on the Bench for fourteen years and wrote
more than a thousand opinions which Bruce R. Trimble, his bio-
grapher, doubts will ever be equalled. Chief Justice Waite:
Defender of the Public Interest (Princeton: Princeton University
Press, 1938), p. 271.

[8]G. Edward White, The American Judicial Tradition, p. 200.
See S. Sidney Ulmer, "The Use of Power in the Supreme Court: The
Opinion Assignments of Earl Warren, 1953-1960," 19 Journal of
Public Law, 49-67 (1970). But while the Chief Justice is primus
inter pares he is not the sole or even the dominant source of
power. Thus, despite the popular image of an activist Warren Court
and Warren's commanding influence, there was a good deal of dis-
sent on his Court, in fact more dissents than usual during these
years. Moreover, it must be remembered that all told seventeen
Justices sat on the sixteen years of the Warren Court and only
Black and Douglas were with the Chief Justice the whole time.
Joseph W. Bishop, "The Warren Court is Unlikely to be Overruled,"
The New York Times Magazine, September 7, 1969, p. 31. It was
Justice Miller's view on the Waite Court (1874-88) that the Chief
Justice exerts additional power only when his character and quali-
fications "would give him a controlling influence without the
position." C. Peter Magrath, Morrison R. Waite: The Triumph of
Character, p. 251.

[9]Merlo J. Pusey, Charles Evans Hughes (New York: Macmillan Co., 1952), II, p. 678. Elliot E. Slotnick who studied the alternative opinion processes of the state courts quotes Justice Kingsley of California that when an "expert" arises, the other Justices defer to him "with the result that a one man, rather than a full court opinion will get filed." "Who Speaks For the Court? The View From the States," 26 Emory Law Journal 112 (1977). Justice Powell who once supported the "expert" approach now rejects it. See ch. IV, n. 3. In the Taft Court (1921-30), however, there was a good deal of assignments based on expertise with Justice Clarke doing patent cases, Brandeis doing tax and rate litigation cases, Van Devanter doing land claims and Indian litigation cases, and Sutherland doing cases involving boundary lines, water rights, and irrigation projects. Patent cases were especially burdensome, heavily technical and "so complicated" that Chief Justice Taft's colleagues had taken the extraordinary step of not voting but leaving the disposition wholly to Taft's discretion. "We very rarely do such a thing as this in our Court," he explained, "but the character of the case is such, with the length of the record, that it is difficult to do otherwise. It is a very common thing in most supreme courts to refer a case to one judge and let him work it out. We never or certainly very rarely, do that." Alpheus Thomas Mason, William Howard Taft: Chief Justice (New York: Simon and Schuster, 1965), p. 206.

[10]Merlo J. Pusey, "Mr. Chief Justice Hughes," in Allison Dunham and Philip B. Kurland, Mr. Justice (Chicago: University of Chicago Press, Phoenix Books, 1964), p. 161.

[11]David J. Danelski, "The Influence of the Chief Justice in the Decisional Process," in Walter F. Murphy and C. Herman Pritchett, Court, Judges, and Politics: An Introduction to the Judicial Process (2nd ed. New York: Random House, 1974), p. 531.

[12]Leon Friedman and Fred L. Israel, The Justices of the United States Supreme Court 1789-1969 Their Lives and Major Opinions, II p. 1480 and III, p. 2114. Merlo J. Pusey, Charles Evans Hughes, II, pp. 677-678. Nina Totenberg, "Behind the Marble, Beneath the Robes," The New York Times Magazine, March 16, 1975, p. 64.

[13]James E. Clayton, The Making of Justice: The Supreme Court in Action (New York: E. P. Dutton, 1964), p. 68.

[14]G. Edward White, The American Judicial Tradition, p. 340.

[15]David W. Rohde and Harold J. Spaeth, Supreme Court Decision Making, p.173. S. Sidney Ulmer's study of assignments in the Warren Court were not all that balanced. Frankfurter was continuously slighted. "The Use of Power in the Supreme Court:

The Opinion Assignments of Earl Warren, 1953-1960," 19 <u>Journal of Public Law</u>, 53-54 (1970).

[16]Anthony Lewis, "A Talk with Warren on Crime, the Court, the Country." <u>The New York Times Magazine</u>, October 19, 1969, p. 130. Perhaps the Court today is more passive and compliant than formerly but there are instances of Justices requesting the Chief Justice: "Two Saturdays in succession you have not assigned me any case but have assigned cases and important ones to Justice Gray. I was in the majority in each case assigned him . . . I am in good health and wish to do my full share." Elliot Slotnick, "Who Speaks For the Court? The View From the States," 26 <u>Emory Law Journal</u> 121 (1977). It is accepted practice that a Justice must write the opinion in the case assigned him unless that Chief Justice withdraws it. "Beyond the Chief Justice's recognition of individual differences lies the 'political' dimensions of the opinion assignment process. Opinion assignments may reflect a concern of the Chief Justice with the ideology of the opinion writer, the alignment of Justices in a case, or other aspects of specific case division." Elliot Slotnick, <u>Ibid.</u>, 123. See Alpheus Thomas Mason, <u>Harlan Fiske Stone, Pillar of the Law</u>, pp. 602-603. Two chronic complainers over assignments were Justice Field. and Justice Clifford on the Waite Court. Justice Field: complained he did not get his share of significant opinions and Justice Clifford, whose mental powers were rapidly declining, frequently rejected assignments. Justice Strong rebelled against writing another opinion on municipal bonds. C. Peter Magrath, <u>Morrison R. Waite: The Triumph of Character</u> (New York: Macmillan, 1963), pp. 257-261.

[17]<u>Korematsu v. United States</u>, 323 U.S. 214 (1944); <u>Abington School District v. Schempp</u>, 374 U.S. 203 (1963); Merlo J. Pusey, <u>Charles Evans Hughes</u>, II, p. 697. Henry J. Abraham, <u>The Judiciary: The Supreme Court in the Governmental Process</u> (3rd ed. Boston: Allyn & Bacon, 1973), p. 35. See S. Sidney Ulmer, "The Analysis of Behavior Patterns on the United States Supreme Court," 22 <u>The Journal of Politics</u>, 642 (1960).

[18]<u>Powell v. Alabama</u>, 287 U.S. 45 (1932); G. Edward White, <u>The American Judicial Tradition</u>, p. 213. John P. Frank, <u>Marble Palace: The Supreme Court in American Life</u>, p. 77. Edwin McElwain, "The Business of the Supreme Court as Conducted by Chief Justice Hughes," in A. Wildavsky and Nelson W. Polsby, <u>American Governmental Institutions</u> (Chicago: Rand McNally, 1968), p. 263. Consult Eloise C. Snyder, "The Supreme Court as a Small Group," 36 <u>Social Forces</u> 232-238 (1958) for a brief study based on a Ph.D. thesis, "A Quantitative Analysis of Supreme Court Opinions from 1921 to 1953," which looks at the Court as a small group divided into subgroups or cliques of Justices. She finds that: (a) the liberal clique was in a state of "readiness" to accept "new" constitutional interpretations: (b) the conservative clique was in a

VRJC LIBRARY

state of "reluctance;" (c) the third clique was the "pivotal" one
and "considered to have had the greatest amount of effective
power;" (d) there was little relationship between the cliques of
Justices and the particular ideologies of the appointing president;
(e) most justices were relatively consistent members of a specific
clique but when switching took place it was more likely from
liberal to conservative rather than the reverse; and (f) as the
conceptual framework of the Court changed points of view and labels
such as "liberal" and "conservative" changed. Chief Justice
Morrison Waite deliberately passed over assigning a case to Justice
Field who it was believed was too close to the railroad interests.
The Chief Justice assigned the opinion, instead, to a "radical,"
David Davis (the National Labor Reform Party nominee for President
in 1872) a practice of Chief Justice Hughes much later of assigning
whenever possible "Justices to write conservative opinions and conservative Justices to write liberal opinions in order to preserve
the Court's image of impartiality." C. Peter Magrath, Morrison R.
Waite: The Triumph of Character (New York: Macmillan, 1963), p. 258.

[19]McDonald v. Santa Fe Transportation Co., 427 U.S. 273
(1976). Henry J. Abraham, Freedom and the Court: Civil Rights and
Liberties in the United States (3rd ed. New York: Oxford University
Press, 1976), p. 390.

[20]Smith v. Allwright, 321 U.S. 649 (1944).

[21]Alpheus Thomas Mason, Harlan Fiske Stone: Pillar of the
Law, p. 615. The remainder of Jackson's letter reads: "I know that
every one of these things is a consideration that to you is distasteful and they are things which I mention only with the greatest
reluctance and frank fear of being misunderstood. I have told
Mr. Justice Frankfurter that in my opinion it is best for this
Court and for him that he should not be its spokesman in this
matter and that I intend to bring my view of it to your attention.
With all humility I suggest that the Court's decision, bound to
arouse bitter resentment, will be much less apt to stir ugly
reactions if the news that the white primary is dead, is broken
to it, if possible, by a Southerner who has been a Democrat and is
not a member of one of the minorities which stir prejudices kindred
to those against the Negro. I have talked with some of them (the
other Justices) who are still in the building, and they feel as I
do." It might be mentioned that the Justices discuss cases with
one another by memos, at lunch, and over the phone - a private line
that does not go through the switchboard. Mary Ann Harrold, Equal
Justice Under Law: The Supreme Court in American Life, p. 138-139.

[22]Samuel Krislov, The Supreme Court in the Political Process
(New York: Macmillan, 1965), p. 62. William P. McLaughlin,
"Research Note: Ideology and Conflict in Supreme Court Opinion
Assignment 1946-1962," 25 Western Political Quarterly, 16-17 (1972)

observes that one of the functions of the opinion assigner is to reduce Court tensions born of ideological positions and is usually done in one of the following ways: (a) "by the choice of the opinion writer . . .;" (b) assignment to a writer "who is ideologically in the center of the majority . . .;" (c) selection of an opinion writer ". . . to have the Court express a consistent ideological view in some kinds of cases . . .;" and (d) the assigner can select himself or someone else close to him ". . . if he wanted to have his own views encompassed by the opinion." McLaughlin's research did indicate that assignment strategies can minimize or eliminate ". . . the general cohesion levels maintained for purposes of the Court's continued operation." Ibid., p. 27.

[23]G. Edward White, The American Judicial Tradition, p. 195. See Walter F. Murphy and C. Herman Pritchett, Courts, Judges, and Politics for Chief Justice William H. Taft's confidential memorandum on asking Justice McKenna to step down because he was not mentally vigorous for the work, p. 17. Also see Alpheus Thomas Mason, William Howard Taft: Chief Justice, pp. 213-215. For a pertinent discussion of Justice Oliver W. Holmes's overstay on the Court see Theodore Voorhees "The Resignation of Justice Holmes" (Part 1) 63 American Bar Association Journal, 260-263 (February, 1977) and "The Resignation of Justice Holmes" (Part 2), Ibid., 426-428 (March, 1977). Before Justice William O. Douglas resigned from the Court, November, 1975, his fellow Justices quietly denied him the authority to write majority opinions in which he might cast a tie-breaking vote. Time, April 11, 1977, p. 80. James F. Simon, Independent Journey, pp. 447-449. Earlier the Taft Court resorted to the same strategem regarding Justice Joseph McKenna who was ill and senile. In November, 1924, at a meeting in Chief Justice Taft's house, it was agreed not to decide cases in which McKenna's vote was crucial. Alpheus Thomas Mason, William Howard Taft: Chief Justice (New York: Simon and Schuster, 1965), p. 214. Justice Ward Hunt who sat between 1873 and 1882 had had a paralytic stroke, December 23, 1878, and for four years that he remained a member of the Court, he never sat with his colleagues and never wrote an opinion. He refused to resign without the security of some kind of pension. Chief Justice Morrison Waite who was under a great burden with a short-manned Court finally convinced Congress to pass a pension act whereupon Justice Hunt promptly resigned. Bruce R. Trimble, Chief Justice Waite: Defender of the Public Interest (Princeton: Princeton University Press, 1938), p. 264. If Justice Van Devanter had "pen paralysis" Justice Holmes was a "wonder." Holmes was eighty-five years old but turned out opinions with astonishing rapidity. The only thing that tries him, the Chief Justice observed, "is not to be able to announce the opinion assigned to him on one Saturday night on a week from the following Monday." Alpheus Thomas Mason, William Howard Taft: Chief Justice (New York: Simon & Schuster, 1965), p. 208.

[24]Merlo J. Pusey, Charles Evans Hughes, II p. 667. Similarly, Chief Justice Morrison Waite wrote: "My Dear Swayne: It was an imposition to ask you to take the French . . . case. Send it back to me and I will write it. I shall have plenty of time this week," Bruce R. Trimble, Chief Justice Waite: Defender of the Public Interest, p. 265. During the eight full terms of the Taft Court, Van Devanter wrote only ninety-one opinions but the Chief Justice, William H. Taft wrote two hundred and forty-nine. See Alpheus Thomas Mason, William Howard Taft: Chief Justice, p. 208.

[25]John P. Frank, Marble Palace: The Supreme Court in American Life, p. 77.

[26]Bruce E. Fein, Significant Decisions of the Supreme Court, 1974-75 (Washington, D.C., American Enterprise Institute for Policy Research, 1976), p. 4. James F. Simon, Independent Journey, the Life of William O. Douglas (New York: Penquin Books, 1981), p. 449.

[27]Henry J. Abraham, The Judicial Process: An Introductory Analysis to the Courts of the United States, England, and France, p. 209. Opinion writing and assignments, of course, are strategic as well as rational and while the influence of ideology and attitudes are not unimportant, David Rohde, "Policy Goals, "Strategic Choice and Majority Opinion Assignments on the United States Supreme Court," 16 Midwest Journal of Political Science, 659-661 (1972) notes three important differences between the motivations of elected officials and unelected Justices. One, the Court is a policy forming body but has no electoral responsibility and is virtually independent of an effective removal power; two, the desire for a higher office can influence their judicial behavior; and, three, it has the final "say-so" on matters, for the most part, before it. As an example of constraints on the President, if Congress chooses to utilize them, see Joseph F. Menez, "Presidential Limitations," 74 Queen's Quarterly, 280-293 (Summer, 1967).

[28]David W. Rohde and Harold J. Spaeth, Supreme Court Decision Making, p. 175. David W. Rohde, "Policy Goals, Strategic Choice, and Majority Opinion Assignments in the United States Supreme Court," 16 Midwest Journal of Political Science, 652-682 (1972) argues that the opinion assigner will assign the majority opinion to himself or to the Justice whose position is closest to him on the issue. This hypothesis is not supported by the study of Gregory James Rathjen, "Policy Goals, Strategic Choice, and Majority Opinion Assignments in the United States Supreme Court: A Replication," 18 The American Journal of Political Science, 713-724 (1974). While Rohde studied all civil liberties cases in the Warren Court from 1953 to 1969, Rathjen studied all economic cases decided by the Warren Court from 1958 to 1969.

[29]Joel B. Grossman and Richard S. Wells, Constitutional Law and Judicial Policy Making (New York: John Wiley & Sons, 1972), p. 142. John P. Frank, Marble Palace: The Supreme Court in American Life, p. 120. Perhaps opinions are negotiated because extremes aside or the right and left, it is difficult, if not impossible, to predict with certainty what the middle Justices will do and this is because we cannot tell in advance the premise an individual Justice will assume when making his decision. See Arthur Selyn Miller, "On the Choice of Major Premises in Supreme Court Opinions," 14 Journal of Public Law, 251 (1965) reprinted in Miller's The Supreme Court Myth and Reality (Westport: Greenwood Press, 1978), pp. 105-131. Justice Felix Frankfurter wrote: "The Court's opinions often disclose merely the surface of the judicial process. The compromises that an opinion may embody, the collaborative effort that it may represent, the inarticulate considerations that may have influenced the grounds in which the case went off, the shifts in position that may precede final adjudication - these and like factors cannot, contemporaneously at all events, be brought to the surface." 63 Harvard Law Review 1 (1949). See the discussion on "bargaining" in Walter F. Murphy Elements of Judicial Strategy (Chicago: University of Chicago Press, 1965), 56-68, 198.

[30]Erie Railroad Co. v. Tompkins, 304 U.S. 64 (1938).

[31]Swift v. Tyson, 16 Pet. 1 (1842).

[32]Merlo J. Pusey, Charles Evans Hughes, II p. 711.

[33]Henry J. Abraham, The Judicial Process, p. 206. S. Sidney Ulmer, "The Analysis of Behavior Patterns on the United States Supreme Court" 22 The Journal of Politics, 642 (1960) asserts that in addition to spreading the caseload among the Justices, the Chief Justice has other purposes in his assigning role such as "public relations" and "rewards."

[34]David J. Danelski, "The Influence of the Chief Justice in the Decisional Process" in Walter F. Murphy and C. Herman Pritchett, Courts, Judges, and Politics, p. 530.

CHAPTER VI

WRITING AND OPINION

Writing an opinion is laborious as well as artful, for, as Rufus Choate once observed: "You cannot drop the Greek alphabet and pick up the Iliad."[1] It frequently happens that the Justice writing the opinion will not backtrack on his style or statements - despite discontent with his terminology, content, or structure, what Justice Oliver W. Holmes called "pulling out all the plums and leaving all the dough"[2]-and thus the Justices write concurring opinions. "If you wish to write, placing the case on the ground which I think tenable and desirable", wrote Chief Justice Harlan Stone to Justice Felix Frankfurter, "I shall cheerfully join you. If not, I will add a few observations myself."[3] In a similar instance but this time to Justice Owen Roberts, Chief Justice Stone's memorandum points out how close the two of them are, indicates why and then adds: "If you feel that you could agree with me, I think you would find no difficulty in making some changes in your opinion which would make it unnecessary for me to say anything."[4] On one occasion, Justice Oliver W. Holmes sent Chief Justice Melville Fuller two decisions - one each way![5] On a different occasion, Justice Holmes, less carefree and more complaining, wrote to Harold Laski, the British political theorist. He explained that he had written an opinion in terms to suit the majority of the brethren, although he himself was not in agreement with these terms:

> Years ago I did the same thing in the
> interest of getting a job done. I let
> the brethren put in a reason that I
> thought bad and cut out all that I
> thought good and I have squirmed ever
> since, and swore that never again - but
> again I yield and now comes a petition
> for rehearing pointing out all the
> horrors that will ensure from just what
> I didn't want to say.[6]

Less elegantly but more forcefully, Justice Holmes noted the pressure to yield when he remarked: ". . . the boys generally cut one of the genitals . . ." from his opinion.[7]

The practical effect of a concurring opinion is to detract from or weaken the force of the majority opinion.[8] Its message is often scattered, sometimes diluted and occasionally extraneous. In a most unusual instance, Justice William Brennan first wrote the Court's opinion and then in order to give himself more scope than the majority opinion afforded, wrote an additional concurring opinion, observing: ". . . it cannot be suggested that in cases where the author is the mere instrument of the Court he must forego expression of his own convictions."[9]

Some critics of concurrences feel that they ought not to be used where differences are minor and insignificant. A practice hardly instructive, also, is the frequent use of opinion concurring in part and dissenting in part, opinions that exhibit an image of fragmentation, uncertainty, and shaky legal underpinnings. Thus, the per curiam opinion in the Federal Election Campaign Act case Buckley v. Valeo[10] (1976), covers on the majority and minority side nearly 290 pages with only three Justices able to agree with all portions of the ruling.[11] The Pentagon Papers case[12] and the capital punishment case[13] each featured nine opinions, and Reapportionment case[14] and the 1973 Abortion Cases,[15] each had six, as did the "reverse discrimination" case.[16] This plethora of concurring opinions borders on the seriatim opinions that John Marshall successfully discontinued in order to strengthen the Court.[17] "The practice of writing separate opinions may be valuable and intriguing," writes Henry Abrahams, "yet it hardly lends itself to certainty in the judicial process."[18] John Frank feels that Frankfurter illustrates the overuse of concurrences. Not only are they rarely cited, he observes, but they were a waste of energy.[19] By contrast, John Marshall Harlan, I, spent 34 years on the Court, participated in 14,226 cases, and wrote concurrences in only 27.[20]

Any Justice is expected to write a number of drafts in order to keep his majority intact. Putting five Justices under one umbrella is no mean trick. This often suggests, of course, that the opinion is not what the writer necessarily wanted but what he ended up with.[21] An extreme instance of an opinion re-writing can be found in the writings of Justice Louis Brandeis. Among his papers after his death there was found the thirty-fourth draft of an opinion.[22] Justice William Brennan once circulated ten printed drafts as did Lewis Powell.[23] Such concern in drafting is due in part to

a Justice's oath, said Justice John Marshall Harlan for
". . . each member of the Court must decide each case
as if he were its own judge."[24]

Drafts of opinions - called "slip opinions" - are
printed in the high security printing room in the Court
building and are numbered so as to keep track of them.[25]
After the printing, in Justice Benjamin Cardozo's
phrase, "the fur begins to fly."[26] Justices discuss by
memoranda, at lunch, and over the phone - a private
line that does not go through the switchboard. Notwithstanding this contact, however, the Justices work
pretty much in isolation, except as they choose to consult or write memos to one another. Actually the
Justices are together only twice, at the public session
when hearing oral arguments and in their secret conferences.[27] As Justice Lewis Powell observed: "We
function as nine small, independent law firms."[28]

Drafting an opinion is not a process but an event,
said Justice Lewis Powell. What he found disturbing
was a cryptic note from a Justice merely saying: "I
will wait circulation of the dissent."[29] A Justice
might write on a slip opinion, as it was done in the
Taft Court, "I shall acquiesce in silence unless someone else dissents."[30] Justice Brandeis once circulated
a dissent in the Taft Court and withdrew it after he
was able to make changes in the majority opinion.[31]
This practice, of course, has the tendency to accent
individuality rather than collegiality. The Justice
becomes, in Justice Robert Jackson's words, "the keeper
of his own conscience."[32]

Switching is not unusual and it has not infrequently occurred that Justices, on the basis of dissents, have changed sides. The Court is a collegial
body and, of course, the Justices influence one another.
No Justice starts out from an absolutely fixed position. In a case which concerned an anti-doorbell
ringing ordinance, Justice Hugo Black switched as a
result of Justice Murphy's dissent and then wrote the
opinion which upheld the view that the ordinance violated religious freedom.[33] Once on the basis of information that Justice Harlan Stone furnished Chief
Justice William H. Taft, the Chief Justice wrote: "I
think we made a mistake in this case and have written
the opinion the other way." His view became the
opinion of the Court.[34]

In another instance, Justice William O. Douglas

voted against rabble-rouser Terminiello, and then
changed his mind and supported him in Terminiello v.
Chicago.[35]   Justice William Brennan converted more than
one of his proposed majority opinions into a dissent
before the final decision was announced and "had the
more satisfactory experience of rewriting a dissent as
a majority opinion for the Court."[36]   Justice Robert
Jackson had changed his vote and said so from the
bench: ". . . I am as stubborn as most . . ." he said.
"But sometimes wind up not voting the way I voted in
conference because the reasons of the majority didn't
satisfy me."[37]   In the first big school busing case,
Swann v. Charlotte-Mecklenburg County Board of Education[38] (1971), Chief Justice Warren Burger wrote a
unanimous opinion for a Court that had switched and
somersaulted. The first vote was 6 to 3 against busing
and, following John Marshall Harlan's pro-school busing
opinion - three Justices changed their minds and voted
6 to 3 for busing. Chief Justice Burger, Harry Blackmun
and Hugo Black dissented. In an about face the three
dissents joined the majority, and Chief Justice Burger,
who had anticipated writing the Court's opinion against
busing, now wrote it for a majority Court in favor of
busing.[39]   In O'Connor (1975) Chief Justice Burger
decided to write the majority opinion, and Justice
Potter Stewart, the concurring opinion. When he circulated his slip opinion, the Chief Justice lost his
majority, and Justice William O. Douglas, the senior
Justice of the new majority, offered it to Justice
Stewart who wrote the majority opinion. Chief Justice
Warren Burger then wrote a concurring opinion.[40]

       Emotional appeals occasionally are made to the
Court of patriotism, or to a "sensed fear that a Justice
may have of being isolated."[41]   Thus, just as he was
about to write a dissent in the Japanese Relocation
cases, Justice Frank Murphy switched[42] to a concurrence
when Justice Felix Frankfurter made a strong plea.[43]
On a church and state issue Justice Frankfurter wrote
to Justice Murphy: "You have a chance to do for your
country and your church such as never come to you
before - and may never come again."[44]

       Although the Justices were unanimous in Ex parte
Quirin[45] (1942) that the Government could try the Nazi
saboteurs in military tribunals, their reasons were
unclear. Justice Frank Murphy quoted an unnamed
Justice's letter to his brethren urging them to vote
unanimously, which they did, and to try the "damned
scoundrels" inasmuch as our fighting men - and many of

them lawyers, were risking their necks for the Republic.[46] The crucial variable in a Supreme Court opinion, as Francis Biddle put it, "may be the judge himself" and

> His views may flow from deeply rooted personal values, from subconscious biases or intuitive judgments, from the influence exerted by his brethren in a collegial situation, and from his own notion of what is appropriate for the Supreme Court to do in a particular instance.[47]

NOTES

CHAPTER VI

[1]Tom C. Clark, "The Supreme Court Conference," in Alan
Weston, The Supreme Court: View From Inside (W. W. Norton & Co.,
1961), p. 49.

[2]Joseph F. Menez in Paul C. Bartholomew, Summaries of Leading
Cases on the Constitution (Totowa, N.J.: Littlefield, Adams and
Co., 1981, 11th ed.) revised by Joseph F. Menez, p. 1-8. Walter
Schaefer of the Illinois Supreme Court emphasized that "opinions
do not all have the same value" even to the writer. In close cases
one convinces himself "as Cardozo once said, 51 percent, and then
you write an opinion that indicates you are convinced in varying
degrees from somewhere in the 40 percent area up to somewhere in
the 70 percent range. The opinion that emerges is the opinion of
the court, but it is actually a very close decision, not to be
stretched, not to be expanded, and not to be distorted." Robert L.
Stern and Eugene Gressman, Supreme Court Practice, p. 713 note 20.

[3]Sheldon Goldman and Thomas P. Jahnige, The Federal Courts
as a Political System, p. 176.

[4]Walter F. Murphy and C. Herman Pritchett, Courts, Judges,
and Politics, p. 518.

[5]William L. King, Melville Weston Fuller: Chief Justice of
the United States 1888-1910, p. 319. Once when Justice Whittaker
had trouble writing the majority opinion in a five to four case,
he solicited help from Justice Douglas who had already written a
dissent. Douglas wrote the majority draft "and when the opinion
came down (Meyer v. United States 364 U.S. 410) it was one of the
few in which the majority and minority opinions were written by
the same man." The Court Years 1939-1975, p. 173.

[6]James MacGregor Burns, J. W. Peltason, and Thomas E. Cronin,
Government by the People, (9th ed. Englewood Cliffs: Prentice-Hall,
1975), p. 416.

[7]Walter F. Murphy and Michael N. Danielson, Carr and
Bernstein's American Democracy (Hinsdale: The Dryden Press, 1977),
p. 405.

[8]Even a majority opinion might not accord with the views of
the authors as in Abbate v. United States, 359 U.S. 187 (1959).
Justice William J. Brennan was assigned this case which involved
double jeopardy and although he got a majority of five, he could
not persuade them of all his views and thus proceeded "to write
a separate concurring opinion." David W. Rohde and Harold J. Spaeth,

Supreme Court Decision Making, p. 189 note 2. "Burger v. Warren -
Whose Court is Better?" United States News & World Report,
March 7, 1977, p. 66. In Barr v. Matteo, 360 U.S. 564 (1959),
Justice Hugo Black assigned the opinion and chose a member of the
Frankfurter bloc. But while this led to an opinion to which the
other block members subscribed, it did not satisfy Black himself.
Thus we see an assigning Justice writing a concurring opinion
expressing his own views for as Black said: ". . . they are not
altogether the same as those stated in the opinion of Mr. Justice
Harlan." See S. Sidney Ulmer, "The Analysis of Behavior Patterns
on the United States Supreme Court" 22 The Journal of Politics
649 (1960).

[9]Henry J. Abraham, The Judicial Process, p. 213.

[10]Buckley v. Valeo, 424 U.S. 1 (1976).

[11]Rowland L. Young, "Supreme Court Report," 62 American Bar
Association Journal, 362 (March, 1976).

[12]The New York Times v. United States, 403 U.S. 713 (1971).

[13]Furman v. Georgia, 408 U.S. 238 (1972).

[14]Baker v. Carr, 369 U.S. 186 (1962).

[15]Roe v. Wade, 410 U.S. 113 (1973); Doe v. Bolton, 410 U.S.
197 (1973).

[16]Regents of the University of California v. Bakke, 438
U.S. 265 (1978).

[17]Edward Corwin, "John Marshall," in Edward T. James, The
American Plutarch (New York: Charles Scribners, 1964), p. 164.
Thomas Jefferson detected the change to a "monolithic" court when
he wrote about Marshall and his Court: "An opinion is huddled up
in conclave, perhaps by a majority of one, delivered as though
unanimous and with the silent acquiescence of lazy or timid
associates, by a crafty Chief Judge, who sophisticates the law
to his mind, by the turn of his own reasoning . . ." Fred Rodell,
"It Is the Earl Warren Court," The New York Times Magazine
March 13, 1966, p. 28. "Mr. Jefferson," writes Justice Robert
Jackson, "would have required each Justice to write his reasons
in every case, as proof that he gave it consideration and did not
merely follow a leader," The Supreme Court in the American System
of Government (New York: Harper & Row, Harper Torchbooks, 1955),
p. 17. Hylton v. United States, 3 Dallas 171 (1796) is an example
of a seriatim opinion. So forceful was Chief Justice John
Marshall in abolishing the seriatim practice in the interest of
centralizing the position of Chief Justice that it took years for
William Johnson to establish the right to dissent without it

appearing to "most of his colleagues as almost treasonable."
Samuel Krislov, The Supreme Court in the Political Process (New
York: Macmillan, 1965), p. 56. Justice Johnson told Thomas
Jefferson: "While I was on the state bench I was accustomed to
delivering seriatim opinions . . . and was not a little surprised
to find our Chief Justice delivering all the opinions in cases in
which he sat, even in some instances when contrary to his own
judgment and vote. But I remonstrated in vain; the answer was he
was willing to take the trouble." Walter F. Murphy, Elements of
Judicial Strategy, p. 40.

[18]Henry J. Abraham, The Judicial Process, p. 210. "Concurring opinions were unusual in the early history of the Court
and uncommon until the beginning of World War Two. While one such
opinion is reported as early as 1797, there were no concurring
opinions as late as the regular terms of 1924 and 1925." Albert P.
Blaustein and Roy M. Mersky, The First One Hundred Justices, p. 95.

[19]John P. Frank, Marble Palace: The Supreme Court in American
Life, p. 126. Sidney Ulmer suggests that it is likely that Frank-
furter resorted to writing concurrences because of the discrimi-
nation practiced by the Chief Justice in opinion assignments.
S. Sidney Ulmer, "The Use of Power in The Supreme Court; the
Opinion Assignments of Earl Warren, 1953-1960," 19 Journal of
Public Law, 53 (1970).

[20]Alan F. Westin, "Mr. Justice Harlan," in Allison Dunham
and Philip B. Kurland, Mr. Justice (Chicago: University of Chicago
Press, Phoenix Books, 1964), p. 117.

[21]James McGregor Burns, J. W. Peltason, and Thomas E. Cronin,
Government by the People, p. 114.

[22]David W. Rohde and Harold J. Spaeth, Supreme Court Decision
Making, p. 69.

[23]William J. Brennan, Jr., "Inside View of the High Court,"
in Leonard W. Levy, The Supreme Court Under Earl Warren (New York:
New York Times Co., Quadrangle Books, 1972), p. 44. J. Harvie
Wilkinson, Serving Justice: A Supreme Court Clerk's View (New York:
Charterhouse, 1974), pp. 76, 92.

[24]Mary Ann Harrell, Equal Justice Under Law: The Supreme
Court in American Life, p. 10.

[25]Glen Elsasser and Jack Fuller, "The Hidden Face of the
Supreme Court," Chicago Tribune, April 23, 1978, Sect. 9, p. 18.
Anthony Lewis, The Supreme Court and How It Works (New York:
Random House, 1966), p. 46.

[26]Tom Clark, "The Supreme Court Conference," in Alan Westin, The Supreme Court: Views From Inside (New York: W. W. Norton, 1961), p. 49.

[27]John Osborne, "One Supreme Court," in Leon I. Solomon, The Supreme Court (New York: H. W. Wilson, The Reference Shelf, Vol. 33, No. 1, 1961), p. 18.

[28]Lewis F. Powell, "What the Justices are Saying," 62 American Bar Association Journal 1454 (November, 1976). Said Justice Robert Jackson: "The fact is that the Court functions less as one deliberative body than as nine, each Justice working largely in isolation except as he chooses to seek consultation with others. These working methods tend to cultivate a highly individualistic rather than a group viewpoint." The Supreme Court in the American System of Government, p. 16.

[29]Lewis F. Powell, "What the Justices are Saying," 62 American Bar Association Journal, 1454 (November, 1976).

[30]Alpheus Thomas Mason, Harlan Fiske Stone: Pillar of the Law, p. 252.

[31]Sheldon Goldman and Thomas P. Jahnige, The Federal Courts as a Political System, p. 175.

[32]Robert H. Jackson, The Supreme Court in the American System of Government, p. 16.

[33]Martin v. Struthers, 319 U.S. 141 (1943). J. Woodford Howard, Jr., "On the Fluidity of Judicial Choice," 62 The American Political Science Review 48 (March, 1968). William O. Douglas, The Court Years 1939-1975, p. 45.

[34]Alpheus Thomas Mason, Harlan Fiske Stone: Pillar of the Law, p. 222. Justice Robert Jackson as a member of the Court reversed a position he had assumed while Attorney General of the United States. In the Coronado case, United Mine Workers of America v. Coronado Coal Co., 259 U.S. 344 (1921) Justice Brandeis had circulated a dissent when the Court by a narrow margin had decided that unions were liable under the Sherman Act. After Taft became Chief Justice the case was restored to the docket. There was a reargument and Justice Brandeis sent some suggestions to Chief Justice Taft "all of which," said Taft, "I shall adopt." Brandeis suggestions not only changed Taft's position but that of the whole Court and at the end of the 1921 term, Taft delivered a unanimous opinion which held that labor unions were not liable. "They will take it from Taft but wouldn't take it from me," Brandeis remarked wryly: "If it is good enough for Taft, it is good enough for us, they say - and a natural sentiment."

Alpheus Thomas Mason, <u>William Howard Taft: Chief Justice</u> (New York: Simon and Schuster, 1965), p. 203.

[35]<u>Terminiello v. Chicago</u>, 337 U.S. 1 (1949). J. Woodford Howard, Jr., "On the Fluidity of Judicial Choice," 62 <u>The American Political Science Review</u>, 49 (March, 1968).

[36]William J. Brennan, Jr., "Inside View of the High Court," in Leonard W. Levy, <u>The Supreme Court Under Earl Warren</u>, p. 44.

[37]Walter F. Murphy, <u>Elements of Judicial Strategy</u>, p. 44. Justice Felix Frankfurter's aphorism seems appropriate: "Wisdom too often never comes, and so one ought not to reject it merely because it comes late." Harold J. Spaeth, <u>Supreme Court Policy Making: Explanation and Prediction</u> (San Francisco: W. H. Freeman and Co., 1979), p. 61.

[38]<u>Swann v. Charlotte-Mecklenburg Board of Education</u>, 402 U.S. 1 (1971).

[39]Nina Totenberg, "Conflict at the Court," <u>Washington Magazine</u>, February, 1974, reprinted in <u>Annual Editions, Readings in American Government 1977-78</u> (The Dushkin Publishing Group, Inc., Sluice Dock, Guilford Ct., 1977), p. 144.

[40]<u>O'Connor v. Donaldson</u>, 422 U.S. 563 (1975). Nina Totenberg, "An Inside View of the Supreme Court," <u>The Muncie Star</u>, May 21, 1978, <u>Family Weekly</u>, p. 4.

[41]Walter F. Murphy and C. Herman Pritchett, <u>Courts, Judges, and Politics</u>, p. 515.

[42]<u>Hirabayaski v. United States</u>, 320 U.S. 81 (1943); <u>Korematsu v. United States</u>, 323 U.S. 214 (1944).

[43]Walter F. Murphy, <u>Elements of Judicial Strategy</u>, p. 46.

[44]Sheldon Goldman and Thomas P. Jahnige, <u>The Federal Courts as a Political System</u>, p. 173. Frankfurter's very personal letter began: "You have some false friends - those who flatter you and play on you for their purposes, not for your good." Then he proceeds to flatter Murphy. J. Woodford Howard, Jr., <u>Mr. Justice Murphy: A Political Biography</u> (Princeton: Princeton University Press, 1968), pp. 449-450. It is worth noting that at the same time Frankfurter was urging Murphy to surmount sectarian considerations on Church-State issues, he greatly relied upon the Synagogue Council of America brief in <u>McCollum v. Board of Education</u>, 333 U.S. 203 (1948) which prohibited non-coercive religious teaching in the school building. See Samuel Krislov, "The <u>Amicus Curiae</u> Brief: From Friendship to Advocacy," 72 <u>Yale Law Journal</u>, 711. Also Fowler V. Harper and Elvin D. Etherington,

"Lobbying Before the Court," 101 <u>University of Pennsylvania Law Review</u>, 1174 (1953).

[45]<u>Ex parte Quirin</u>, 317 U.S. 1 (1942). For a discussion see Robert E. Cushman, "The Case of the Nazi Saboteurs," 36 <u>American Political Science Review</u> 1082-1091 and Paul L. Murphy, <u>The Constitution in Crisis 1918-1969</u> (New York: Harper & Row, Torchbooks, 1972), p. 243.

[46]Walter F. Murphy, <u>Elements of Judicial Strategy</u>, pp. 48-49. In <u>Hirabayashi v. United States</u>, 320 U.S. 81 (1943), Justice Felix Frankfurter again pressured Justice Frank Murphy to close ranks with his colleagues arguing: "Please, Frank, with our eagerness for the austere functions of the Court and your desire to do all that is humanly possible to maintain and enhance the corporate reputation of the Court, why don't you take the initiative with the Chief Justice in getting him to take out everything that either offends you or that you would want to express more ironically." <u>Ibid.</u>, 46. Douglas calls Frankfurter a "proselytizer extraordinary," p. 21 and further adds: "Up and down the halls he went, pleading, needling, nudging, probing. He never stopped trying to change the votes on a case until the decision came down." <u>The Court Years 1939-1975</u>, p. 22. Alpheus Thomas Mason, <u>Harlan Fiske Stone: Pillar of the Law</u>, pp. 653-671. See Arthur S. Miller, "On the Need for 'Impact Analysis' of Supreme Court Decisions," 53 <u>Georgetown Law Journal</u> 365 (1965) reprinted in Arthur S. Miller, <u>The Supreme Court: Myth and Reality</u> (Westport, Greenwood Press, 1978), pp. 230-233.

[47]Francis Biddle, "An Inside View of Appointing Supreme Court Justices," in Joel Grossman and Richard S. Wells, <u>Constitutional Law and Judicial Policy Making</u> (New York: John Wiley & Sons, 1972), p. 210.

DISSENTS AND OPINIONS: QUALITY AND QUANTITY

Dissents have had a long, almost a romantic tradition, in which the writer, whatever the cost of being in the minority - must stand fast to his principles. But although a dissent is an appeal to what Chief Justice Charles F. Hughes called ". . . the brooding spirit of the law, to the intelligence of a future day . . .,"[1] still it is not controlling law. The point is, of course, that it will alter the controlling law and in some cases cause its abandonment.

Famous dissents which overturned the majority opinion come to mind easily enough. Justice Oliver W. Holmes dissented in Lochner v. New York[2] (1905), saying, in part, that the majority opinion was founded "upon an economic theory which a large part of the country does not entertain;" in Plessy v. Ferguson[3] (1896) Justice John Marshall Harlan, I, dissented, saying: "Our Constitution is color blind;" in Betts v. Brady[4] (1942), Justice Hugo Black said: "The right to counsel in a criminal proceeding is 'fundamental'"; and in Minersville School District v. Gobitis[5] (1940), Justice Harlan Stone dissented saying: "The guarantees of civil liberty are but guarantees of freedom of the human mind and spirit and of reasonable freedom and opportunity to express them." There are other historic dissents and already a literature of dissent.[6]

The dissent deals with an issue already determined, it is true, but the dissenter seeks to persuade his contemporaries and the future that his colleagues decided it wrongly. Justice Felix Frankfurter, discussing Harris v. United States[7] (1947), said in a memorandum to Justice Frank Murphy: "This is a protest opinion - a protest at the bar of the future - but also an effort to make the brethren realize what is at stake."[8] A dissent, of course, can also push a majority opinion into new and perhaps untenable territory, as in Myers v. United States[9] (1926). After prolonged deliberation and after a second argument, Chief Justice Taft produced a 71-page opinion, but it produced, in turn, a 56-page dissent from Justice Louis Brandeis and a 61-page dissent from Justice James McReynolds. Chief Justice Taft doubled his opinion to cover the points raised in the dissents.[10] Taft's original rendition

"had been twenty-eight pages, but after Brandeis had
filed a dissent of thirty-two pages, and McReynolds
had followed suit with forty-nine pages, the Chief
Justice had to double his in order to cover the points
the dissenters had insisted on developing, a few days
before the opinion went down."[11] It was this experience which weakened "teamwork" that caused Taft to
detest dissents, write few himself, and dissuade anyone
elso from utilizing them. Chief Justice Roger B.
Taney's extreme position in Dred Scott v. Sandford,
(1857), was partly occasioned by Justice John McLean's
extreme dissent.[12]

A Justice has to be aware of his dissents, especially if he dissents often. Chief Justice Stone said to
Karl Llewellyn: "You know, if I should write in every
case where I do not agree with some of the views
expressed in the opinions, you and all my other friends
would stop reading them."[13] Off the "judicial leash,"
the dissent affords an outlet for individuality, independence, and idiosyncrasy.[14] It would be pleasant to
believe that the dissent, furthermore, always or even
often embodies great wisdom or refutes error. Such
is not the case. Style-wise the dissent has a greater
freedom than the majority opinion which closely
reflects the majority viewpoint in expounding the law.
"Because you . . . can go off and express your own view
without regard to anybody else," said Justice Robert
Jackson, "it is more fun to write a dissenting opinion
or a concurring opinion."[15] Chief Justice Harlan Stone,
as much a dissenter as his Court, nevertheless felt it
necessary to warn his colleagues "lest its usefulness
and effectiveness be impaired by its abuse."[16] "An
intriguing but not very hopeful practice," says Henry
Abrahams, is to dissent without an opinion.[17]

The truth is that dissents are rarely cited and
are most often forgotten. Justice John Marshall Harlan,
I, sat on the Court for 34 years and wrote 380 dissents,
but only two have survived as law: Brown v. Board of
Education of Topeka[18] (1954) overruled Plessy v.
Ferguson,[19] (1896) and Heart of Atlanta Motel v. United
States[20] (1964) overruled the Civil Rights Cases[21]
(1883). Dissent over minor matters - as distinguished
from constitutional ones - weakens the Court's prestige
as an institution.[22] Frequent dissent is often viewed
as an obstruction and always viewed as internal dis-
agreement.[23] A dissent, said Justice Robert Jackson,
was a confession of a "failure to convince the writer's
colleagues, and the true test of a judge is his

influence in leading, and not in opposing his court."[24]

An often heard criticism of the Court is that it is trying to decide more cases than it can decide well. The quantity is too much, and the quality is too low - a charge especially made against Douglas. His critics found his "mental processes untidy," that he was impatient as a craftsman, and that his opinions were less and less clear.[25] In his widely ranging and influential critique of the Court, "The Time Chart of the Justices," H. M. Hart says that Court's opinions are written too fast, do not genuinely illuminate the area of law with which they deal, and are losing the respect of lawyers and judges alike.[26] The Court invariably "finds itself in a mind-numbing race with the clock as its adjournment date nears, and rulings must be churned out at a dizzying rate."[27] Of the 129 signed opinions issued in the October, 1978 term, 76 came out in the final two months. The poor quality of opinions creates problems for executive and legislative officials who find they have difficulty in the light of them to plan or to act.[28] A widely read columnist, James Kilpatrick believes the Court is hardly literate,[29] and John Frank, in The Marble Palace, noted that an anthology of some very good things could be put together from 350 volumes of the United States Supreme Court Reports, "but the editor would probably have 348 volumes left over."[30]

In a widely circulted poll of 211 judges of the District and Court of Appeals in addition to 110 justices of state supreme courts and 187 lawyers, the overall rating of Supreme Court opinions was 59.7% or "average." Those polled agreed that 75% of the opinions are often "too long"; 65.3% felt that the opinions are often "unclear," 69.9% claimed they create problems of confusion and misinterpretation, and 84% believed the opinions could and should be shorter. The poll rated the quality of opinions in the Burger Court only slightly higher than that of the Warren Court.[31]

Professor Philip Kurland, a critic of the Court, believes the Court's opinions are approaching, "the danger point" and quotes Professor Harry Kalven, Jr., a friendly critic: "I think that part of the current grievance is the momentum, the haste with which the Court changes; the failure to connect up its current decision with something it has inherited from the past."[32] Wrangling and verbosity are not new on the Court. Justice James McReynolds, Woodrow Wilson's appointee who, in Chief Justice Howard Taft's phrase, has been "spoiled for usefulness," liked brevity and once told Justice Stone to "discuss the essential law point and no others." "Your opinion," he said, about Stone's rambling style, "would be much better if only half as long. Think of the 10,000 who should read what you say."[33] Few Justices have the writing qualities attributed to Chief Justice Charles E. Hughes, those of accuracy, clarity, conciseness, and power, "the four corners of a good judicial craftsmanship."[34]

In fairness, it might be noted, poorly written opinions are not necessarily the result of poor thinking. On occasion, opinions are deliberately written to obscure the point of law. Charles Evans Hughes' opinions were highly polished, but he could alter or cloud them to get a majority.[35] On this point Chief Justice Hughes quoted Justice Holmes: "Justice Holmes used to say, when we asked him to excise portions of his opinions which he thought pretty good, that he was willing to be 'reasonably raped'. I feel the same way."[36] This ambiguity is built into the opinion because not infrequently, in a collegial opinion, terms mean one thing to one Justice and something else to another - so much so that occasionally the writing approaches unintelligibility as in Yamashita[37] and in Jenks.[38] When minor differences cannot be reconciled, as a former law clerk put it, "That's when you fudge it, and then the law professors complain that the Court doesn't write clear opinions. Or else you leave out the point altogether. And then the law professors complain that there is a step missing in the Court's logic."[39] Despite the "plain words" approach to constitutional meaning,[40] the Court does not write all that plainly itself.

CHAPTER VII

[1]Charles Evans Hughes, The Supreme Court of the United States (New York: Columbia University Press, Garden City Publishing Co., 1936), p. 68. The dissenter, says S. Sidney Ulmer, "Analysis of Behavior on the United States Supreme Court," 22 The Journal of Politics, 638 (1960) has a number of choices: Thus (1) he can concur in the result, (2) write a concurring opinion, (3) dissent, (4) write a dissenting opinion, and (5) concur with the concurring, dissenting, or majority opinion.

[2]Lochner v. New York, 198 U.S. 45 (1905).

[3]Plessy v. Ferguson, 163 U.S. 537 (1896).

[4]Betts v. Brady, 316 U.S. 455 (1942).

[5]Minersville School District v. Gobitis, 310 U.S. 586 (1940).

[6]Alan Barth, Prophets with Honor: Great Dissents and Great Dissenters In the Supreme Court (New York: Vintage, 1974). Percival E. Jackson, Dissent in the Supreme Court: A Chronology (Norman: University of Oklahoma Press, 1969).

[7]Harris v. United States, 331 U.S. 145 (1947).

[8]Walter F. Murphy and C. Herman Pritchett, Courts, Judges, and Politics, p. 518. A dissent, of course, can be a symbol and source of argument for those who oppose the Court, may undermine "popular confidence in the Court's authority" and provide fuel for present and future disagreements. David J. Danelski, "Conflict and Its Resolution in the Supreme Court," XI, The Journal of Conflict Resolution, pp. 72-73 (1967).

[9]Myers v. United States, 272 U.S. 52 (1926).

[10]Robert F. Cushman, Cases in Constitutional Law (4th ed. Englewood Cliffs: Prentice-Hall, 1975), p. 121. Knowing that Chief Justice Taft disliked dissents to begin with and long ones even more so, Brandeis offered to pay the cost of printing his dissent out of his own pocket, Alpheus Thomas Mason, William Howard Taft: Chief Justice, p. 225.

[11]Alpheus Thomas Mason, Harlan Fiske Stone: Pillar of the Law, p. 231.

[12]Henry J. Abraham, The Judicial Process, p. 204. Alfred H. Kelly and Winifred A. Harbison, The American Constitution: Its Origins and Development (New York: W. W. Norton, 1948), pp. 385-388. G. Edward White, The American Judicial Tradition, p. 180. Justice Pierce Butler took to the 'no dissent unless absolutely necessary' school when he wrote Chief Justice Taft: "I voted to reverse, while this sustains your conclusion to affirm, I still think reversal would be better. But I shall in silence acquiesce. Dissents seldom aid in the right development of statement of the law. They often do harm. For myself I say: "lead us not into temptation." David J. Danelski, "The Influence of the Chief Justice in the Decisional Process," in Aaron Wildavsky and Nelson W. Polsby, American Government Institutions (Chicago: Rand McNally & Co., 1968), p. 254.

[13]Walter F. Murphy, Elements of Judicial Strategy, p. 62.

[14]Alan Barth, Prophets with Honor: Great Dissents and Great Dissenters in the Supreme Court, p. 4.

[15]Ibid., p. 5.

[16]Alpheus Thomas Mason, Harlan Fiske Stone: Pillar of the Law, p. 608.

[17]Henry J. Abraham, Freedom and the Court: Civil Rights and Liberties in the United States, pp. 55, 112.

[18]Brown v. Board of Education of Topeka, 347 U.S. 483 (1954).

[19]Plessy v. Ferguson, 163 U.S. 537 (1896).

[20]Heart of Atlanta Motel v. United States, 379 U.S. 241 (1964).

[21]Civil Rights Cases, 109 U.S. 3 (1883).

[22]John P. Frank, Marble Palace: The Supreme Court in American Life, pp. 127, 129.

[23]Alpheus Thomas Mason, Harlan Fiske Stone: Pillar of the Law, p. 603.

[24]Robert H. Jackson, The Supreme Court in the American System of Government, p. 19. Walter F. Murphy and C. Herman Pritchett, Courts, Judges, and Politics, p. 518.

[25]Milton Viorst, "Bill Douglas Has Never Stopped Fighting the Bullies of Yakima," The New York Times Magazine, June 14, 1970, p. 8. James F. Simon, Independent Journey: The Life of William O. Douglas says Douglas was simply not interested in

writing scholarly opinions, p. 353.

[26]Henry M. Hart, Jr., "The Supreme Court, 1958 Term; Fore-ward: The Time Chart of the Justices," Harvard Law Review, 84-101, (November, 1959) reprinted in Robert Scigliano, The Courts: A Reader in the Judicial Process (Boston: Little, Brown and Co., 1957), pp. 275-290. Richard Y. Funston, Constitutional Counter-Revolution? The Warren Court and the Burger Court: Judicial Policy Making in Modern America (New York: John Wiley & Sons, 1977), p. 311.

[27]"Supreme Court Trials and Tribulations," United States News and World Report, March 26, 1977, p. 33.

[28]Harold J. Spaeth, An Introduction to Supreme Court Decision Making (Rev. ed. New York: Chandler Publishing Co., 1972), p. 43. The final volume of the Lawyers' Edition covering the 1981-82 term lists 37 cases and not counting, memorandum cases, contains 952 pages. In the final three weeks of the 1981-82 term, moreover, the Court delivered 58 opinions or 40% of the Court's output. If this were not disturbing enough, the Court entered the 1982-83 term with 111 hours of argument time carried over despite the fact it schedules only 160 hours of argument a year. Linda Greenhouse, "No Sign of Relief for an Overloaded Court," The New York Times, August 15, 1982, sect. 4. A consequence of a glutted docket is the use of summary dispositions a fear the Chief Justice feels would lead to a decline in the quality of justice or which introduces production line justice. "Chief Justice Burger's Challenge to Congress," United States News and World Report, February 14, 1983, p. 41. For a full report see Chief Justice Burger's "Report on the State of the Judiciary," 69 American Bar Association Journal, 442-447 (April, 1983). "I recognize, of course, that this Court's expanding docket has increased the pressure to accelerate the disposition process" says Justice Marshall and then criticizes the majority, for, in the very least, in not allowing a brief on the merits. Dissenting in Wyrick v. Fields, 74 L.Ed. 2d 214, 221 (1982). Justice Brennan dissenting in Hutto v. Davis, 70 L.Ed. 2d 556, 565 (1982) bitterly complained of summary dispositions "with the benefit of neither full briefing nor oral argument."

[29]James J. Kilpatrick, "High Court Lacks Literacy," Washington Star, July 5, 1976, reprinted in Peter L. Lewis and Kenneth D. People, The Supreme Court and the Criminal Process: Cases and Comments (Philadelphia: W. B. Saunders Co., 1978), pp. 44-45.

[30]John P. Frank, Marble Palace: The Supreme Court in American Life, p. 143. By 1977 there were 429 volumes of United States Supreme Court Reports and over 34,000 decisions. See Chapter V, "Counting the Opinions" in the statistical work of

Albert P. Blaustein and Roy M. Mersky, The First One Hundred
Justices, pp. 87-102. See Larry C. Berkson, The Supreme Court and
Its Publics (Lexington: D. C. Heath & Co., 1978), pp. 32-33, 46-48
for a chart and discussion of writing skills of the most recent
twenty-one Justices. The study was based on sixty names drawn from
a list of constitutional law professors published by the Association of American Law Schools. At the very top of the best writers
are Robert H. Jackson and John Marshall Harlan and at the bottom
are Harold Burton and Charles Whittaker.

[31]"Burger v. Warren: Whose Court is Better?" United States
News and World Report, March 7, 1977, pp. 58, 67. While opinions
are often long, discursive, and filled with dicta the Court itself-
Rule #40 "Briefs - In General" and Rule #42 "Briefs of an Amicus
Curiae" are expected to be short. The Court likes short petitions
and dislikes unduly long ones and, at the suggestion of several
Justices urged Robert L. Stern and Eugene Gressman authors of
Supreme Court Practice to insert the following in capital letters:
"The most important thing to remember is to keep the petition
short," 472. In Huffman v. Pursue, Ltd., 95 S. Ct. 169 the Court
said: "The brief for appellants does not comply with Rules 39 and
40 of the Court with respect to consciseness, the statement of
questions without unnecessary detail, and the printing of appen-
dices thereto. Accordingly, as provided in paragraph 5 of
Rule 40, the brief of the appellants is hereby stricken. Counsel
for appellants may file a brief complying with the Rules within
20 days of the date of the order. Oral argument will be allowed
only by counsel who have filed briefs that conform to the Rules."
See the discussion in Harold J. Spaeth, Supreme Court Policy
Making: Explanation and Prediction of the Court dealing with
briefs, pp. 26, 27, 48 note 19. An earlier and much narrower poll
of the Court of greater Providence, Rhode Island, was quite critical of the Warren Court in a number of areas. Edward N. Beiser,
"Lawyers Judge the Warren Court," 7 Law and Society Review, 139-
149 (1972-1973).

[32]Philip B. Kurland, "The Court Should Decide Less and
Explain More," The New York Times Magazine, June 9, 1968, p. 124.

[33]Alpheus Thomas Mason, Harlan Fiske Stone: Pillar of the
Law, p. 220. On another occasion the irascible McReynolds remarked
about a "slip" opinion which he did not approve: "This statement
makes me sick." Walter F. Murphy, Elements of Judicial Strategy,
p. 52. Notations on "slip" opinions which provide an avenue of
social access and create a pleasant work relationship are the
words written by Justice Holmes to Chief Justice Taft: "I cling to
my preceptor's hand and follow him through the dark passages to
the light;" or the words of Douglas to Stone: "I heartily agree.
This has the master's real touch;" or Justice Murphy to Chief
Justice Stone: "This seems to me the finest kind of writing and
it is sound too." Ibid., 51.

[34]Merlo J. Pusey, <u>Charles Evans Hughes</u>, II, 679.

[35]Edwin McElwain, "The Business of the Supreme Court as Conducted by Chief Justice Hughes," 63 <u>Harvard Law Review</u>, 5-26 (November, 1949) reprinted in Aaron Wildavsky and Nelson W. Polsby, <u>American Governmental Institutions</u> (Chicago: Rand McNally, 1968), p. 263.

[36]Walter F. Murphy and C. Herman Pritchett, <u>Courts, Judges, and Politics</u>, p. 235.

[37]<u>In re Yamashita</u>, 327 U.S. 1 (1946).

[38]<u>Jencks v. United States</u>, 353 U.S. 657 (1957). Harold J. Spaeth, <u>An Introduction to Supreme Court Decision Making</u>, p. 43.

[39]Nina Totenberg, "Behind the Marble, Beneath the Robes," <u>The New York Times Magazine</u>, March 16, 1975, p. 58.

[40]Henry J. Abraham, <u>Freedom and the Court: Civil Rights and and Liberties in the United States</u>, p. 27. Harold J. Spaeth, <u>An Introduction to the Supreme Court Decision Making</u>, p. 48. On the "plain words" of the Constitution see William Anderson, "The Intention of the Framers: A Note on Constitutional Interpretation," 49 <u>The American Political Science Review</u>, 340-352 (June, 1955). The question of "plain words" and "intent" of the Framers continues to divide scholars. See William F. Harris II, "Bonding Word and Polity: The Logic of American Constitutionalism," 76 <u>The American Political Science Review</u>, 43-44 (March, 1982). Justice Hugo Black told Justice Harry Blackmun never to publicly agonize over a difficult decision. "Always write it as though it's clear as crystal." John A. Jenkins, "A Candid Talk With Justice Blackmun," <u>The New York Times Magazine</u>, February 20, 1983, p. 25. How convenient!

CHAPTER VIII

ORAL ARGUMENT: THE STARS AND THE REGULARS

The Justices are almost unanimous in agreeing that, despite the availability of detailed briefs, how well an argument is presented to the Court often spells the difference between winning and losing. The "first impressions that a judge gets of a case are very tenacious," said Justice John M. Harlan. "They frequently persist into the conference room."[1] Justice Harlan noted also that the Court learns by listening - a fact especially pertinent in his case inasmuch as he was blind during his last six years on the Court.[2] "I suppose that, aside from cases of exceptional difficulty," said Chief Justice Charles E. Hughes, "the impression that a judge has at the close of a full oral argument accords with the conviction which controls his final vote."[3] Most of the Court members, wrote Justice Jackson, rely heavily on oral presentation and form "at least a tentative conclusion from it in a large percentage of cases."[4] The consequence of this truth about the oral argument is that the litigants before the Court are not equal in advocacy, and this is especially true when an expert advocate or the Solicitor General is arguing a case.

This seeming unfairness is built into the procedure, for the Court's own Rule 44.1 encourages advocacy and discourages reading a brief at the bar. Rule 44.1[5] says:

> Oral arguments should undertake to emphasize and clarify the written arguments appearing in the briefs theretofore filed. The Court looks with disfavor on any oral argument that is read from a prepared text.

Unlike in the days of Daniel Webster, John C. Calhoun, and Henry Clay in which the counsel spoke for hours or days, counsel today has one-half hour to present his arguments. During the oral argument the Justices converse with one another. If the neophyte lacks expertise or is pitted against a "star" from one of the large Washington-based firms or the Chief Lawyer from a major interest group such as the NAACP or the ACLU that often practice before the Court, then he is at a considerable disadvantage.[6] Thus, when Chief Justice Earl Warren appointed fifty-two-year-old Abe Fortas, the brilliant Washington Attorney and future Associate Justice of the Supreme Court, to argue the case against Florida, represented by its twenty-three-year-old Assistant Attorney General, Bruce Jacob, it was not much of a contest.[7] One reason why oral argument is important is that a brief, however complete, does not allow the Justice to raise doubts, challenge points, or seek clarifications. Justice Frankfurter once said that the Bench saw itself not as a "dozing audience for the reading of soliloquies, but as a questioning body, utilizing oral argument as a means for exposing the difficulties of a case with a view to meeting them."[8] This Socratic Method of Procedure,[9] as Justice John M. Harlan described it, can develop into the "Felix" problem[10] in which Justices constantly interrupt the counsel and exhaust his allotted time. No matter who the counsel, he might come in for his share of questions. Although he subsequently voted in favor of the lawyer's position, Justice Roberts once quizzed a lawyer until the lawyer fainted in the courtroom.[11] Justice Robert Jackson once said that when he was Solicitor General, he made three arguments in every case:

> First came the one that I planned - as I thought, logical, coherent, complete. Second was the one actually presented - interrupted, incoherent, disjointed, disappointing. The third was the utterly devastating argument that I thought of after going to bed that night.[12]

Still another reason for the oral argument is the place it has in the timetable of the decisional process. During the oral argument there is no still photography, or television or even provision for a closed circuit for overflow crowds. Aside from the public and nine desks set aside for the media and artists, there is no other public coverage--especially television. The Justices often take a tentative vote in conference not too long after the oral argument.[13] For example in one Circuit Court of Appeals on which Justice John M. Harlan temporarily sat it was reported that "the voting on the cases took place each day following the close of the arguments."[14]

While it is axiomatic that even the best lawyer will lose the case that cannot be won, the expert

advocate, especially the Solicitor General and his
office, starts with an advantage denied his adversary.[15]
He is not only part of the Executive branch, but the
Court considers him as an officer of the Court who will
police appeals but, in addition, who will aid the Court
in finding the solution most conducive to the public
interest.[16] Whenever a case is lost in the District
Court or Court of Appeals, it is the Solicitor General
who decides whether or not it will be appealed to the
Supreme Court.[17] The Solicitor General prepares about
one half of all the briefs presented to the Supreme
Court.[18] This means that the Solicitor General's office
is responsible for about 60-90 percent of the oral arguments every year, some of which the Solicitor General
takes himself and some of which are assigned.[19] In
rare but not unusual instances, the Solicitor General
will refuse to appeal a case the government has lost by
a "confession of error,"[20] that is, a brief in which he
concedes that the government's views have been wrong in
one or more aspects of the case. Although the Solicitor
General agreed with the agency, in one instance, that a
case was important, he found the lower court's reasoning
persuasive and would not support a review. "I could not
in good conscience," said the Solicitor General, "sign
a petition either expressly or impliedly representing
that the court below had wrongly decided an important
question of federal law."[21] Thomas Thacher, Solicitor
General under Herbert Hoover, used to tell the Court he
had signed the brief but did not agree with the Government's case.[22] When Federal Judge, Simon E. Sobeloff
was Solicitor General, he refused to endorse the views
of the Administration on a constitutional question,
namely, whether the Government, in a loyalty Board case,
can conceal the identity of the accusers. The petition
to the Supreme Court was signed by the Attorney General
of the United States.[23]

In writing this kind of response the Solicitor
General knows that the attorneys who handled the Government's case below, as well as the federal judge who
decided it, will be infuriated.[24] It is not sufficient
that the Solicitor General believes the Government
would lose the appeal; he must also believe that it is
a respectable argument.[25] The goal of the Solicitor
General, summed up on the plaque outside the Attorney
General's door, reads: "The United States wins its point
whenever justice is done its citizens in the courts."[26]

Because of the vast discretionary[27] powers of the
Solicitor General, his expertise, his knowledge of the

law and his role in developing it and the high regard in which he is held by the Supreme Court, it is no accident that the Solicitor General has been character-ized as the Court's "ninth-and-a-half" member.[28]   Jus-tice Robert Jackson once reported that when he was Solicitor General, a letter addressed simply "Celestial General, Washington, D.C." reached him. The Post Office, he said modestly, had no trouble deciding it was meant for him.[29]

An *amicus curiae* brief can be filed only after an order of the Court or when accompanied by written con-sent of all the parties to the case, and "it shall concisely state the nature of the applicants interest, set forth facts or questions of law that have not been, or reasons for believing that they will not adequately be, presented by the parties, and their relevancy to the disposition of the case."[30] The Court seldom or never denies the Solicitor General the right to appear as an *amicus curiae* and, in fact, often invites him to present a brief.[31] Understandably, the Government's interest to see the orderly development of the law, is more pressing and down the pike more important, than the litigant or *amicus* who wants merely to win the case.

It must be remembered that although each Justice has several clerks, the Court itself does not have a staff, and thus it leans heavily on the Solicitor General for a sophisticated analysis of the constitu-tional question. This easy access to the Court gives the Government a substantial edge in affecting the out-come of any case. The Government is a party or an *amicus curiae* in about 60% of the cases before the Court,[32] and approximately two thirds of the Govern-ment's petitions for certiorari - as against one tenth of all other petitions - are granted.[33] When one notes, then, the power of the Solicitor General to file an *amicus* brief at will or to do so at the Court's invi-tation,[34] to deny a review of a lower Court decision or to prevent an agency from appealing a lower court deci-sion even when it is done on policy grounds, and to accumulate a string of victories before the Court that no private litigant or *amicus* could hope to match, it is no wonder that the Government, more often than not, wins the case. Despite the fact the Justices put a high value on courtroom discourse, oral argument is noticeably only average to mediocre in quality when anyone but the "stars" or the Solicitor General are appearing.[35]

102

A Solicitor General or members of his staff are bound to gauge the behavioral characteristics of the Justices, their moods, and proclivities.[36] Because they have often appeared before the Court, they know the Justices well. There is an easy informality before the Court, but it is largely restricted to the long-practiced professionals, who, on numerous occasions, have jousted with the Justice, but this attitude is not extended to the neophytes who never or, at best, only once or twice, appear before the Court. In the famous Gideon case Justice Brennan said helpfully to Abe Fortas: "You are saying that the right to counsel is assured by the Fourteenth Amendment whether by absorption, incorporation or whatever."[37] Counsel Fortas replied: "Mr. Justice you seem to know me well."[38] In another exchange Justice Black wanted to know why Counsel Fortas was not pushing the argument that the Fourteenth Amendment incorporated the entire Bill of Rights. "Mr. Justice Black," replied Fortas very smoothly, "I like that argument that you have made so eloquently. But I cannot as an advocate make that argument because this Court has rejected it so many times. I hope you never cease making it."[39] By contrast, Bruce Jacob had scarcely a five-minute period when he could talk without interruption, not to mention the trouble he encountered when supporting an unpopular cause. He was also unfamiliar with court nuances. When Justice Black quizzed him on the requirement of counsel to insure a fair trial, Jacob retreated and answered: "I'm sorry, your honor, that was a stupid answer."[40] It would be stretching a point to suggest there is anything like a fraternal bias, and yet it is worth observing that several former Justices' clerks and Solicitors General and Attorneys General make it to the Court.[41] This comprises a known "circle," the nuances of which are intriguing.

CHAPTER VIII

[1]John M. Harlan, "What Part Does the Oral Argument Play in the Conduct of an Appeal?" 41 Cornell Law Quarterly, 7 (1955).

[2]Catherine A. Barnes, Men of the Supreme Court. Profiles of the Justices, (New York: Facts on File, 1978), p. 97 col. 2.

[3]Charles Evans Hughes, The Supreme Court of the United States (New York: Garden City Publishing Co., 1936), p. 61.

[4]Robert H. Jackson, "Advocacy Before the Supreme Court: Suggestions for Effective Case Presentations," 37 American Bar Association Journal, 801, (November, 1951), p. 801.

[5]Robert L. Stern and Eugene Gressman, Supreme Court Practice, p. 1105. The complete Rules of the Court are found at pp. 1073-1116.

[6]Samuel Krislov, "The Amicus Curiae Brief: From Friendship to Advocacy," Yale Law Journal, 707-709 (1963). When Justice Thurgood Marshall headed the legal services of the NAACP as Special Counsel, he undertook thirty-two major cases and won twenty-nine of them and helped to set new law in important areas of civil liberties. See Marshall's capsule biography in Charles Van Doren and Robert McHenry, Webster's American Biographies (Springfield: G. and C. Merriam Co., 1975), pp. 692-693.

[7]The contract between Abe Fortas, the future Justice of the Supreme Court, as counsel for Gideon and Bruce Jacob, counsel for Florida is illuminating. Abe Fortas had gone to Yale Law School and was Editor-in-Chief of the Yale Law Journal. In the thirties, he worked for the Government and associated with rising public figures as Secretary of the Interior, Harold Ickes and the future Justice of the Supreme Court, William O. Douglas. Anthony Lewis described Fortas ". . . as one of the country's outstanding appellate advocates, skilled in the special technique of arguing cases to appellate judges." A friend of Justices Hugo Black, William Brennan, and Chief Justice Earl Warren, Fortas had earlier been appointed by Warren to recommend changes in the Rules of Procedure in federal criminal cases and had also appointed him as Gideon's counsel in forma pauperis, that is to say, at the request of the Court because of the defendent's poverty. Bruce Jacob entered private practice while he was preparing Florida's brief and, soon after, joined the National Guard, got married, moved and, with his bride, traveled weekly 250 miles to Tallahassee in order to work in the law library of the Florida Supreme Court. When he arrived in Washington for the oral argument, he had never seen the Court

at work until the day previous to his appearance. In fact, he had to be admitted to the Supreme Court Bar pro hac vice ("for this occasion") to make his argument. Moreover, for the purpose of this case the Court added another half hour to each side and pitted against the new Assistant Attorney General for Florida, George D. Mentz, the amicus counsel for the American Civil Liberties Union and former Solicitor General, J. Lee Rankin. Anthony Lewis, Gideon's Trumpet (New York: Random House, Vintage Books, 1964), pp. 48-56, 139-166. See the tribute to Justice Fortas made before the special session of the Court by Solicitor General Lee, Attorney General Smith, and Chief Justice Burger. Miscellaneous Proceedings, 74 L. Ed. 2d i-viii (March 29, 1983). It is unfortunate that Bruce Jacob did not prepare for his argument before the Supreme Court as did the Assistant Attorney General of Arizona. Jacob might have lost, in fact, he would likely have lost with such a bad case, but it would have been a more interesting contest. See Russell A. Kolsrud, "Preparing for a Supreme Court Argument . . . Do What Your Mother Told You," 66 American Bar Association Journal, 855 (July, 1980).

[8]Ibid., 162.

[9]John Marshall Harlan, "What Part Does the Oral Argument Play in the Conduct of an Appeal?" 41 Cornell Law Quarterly, 7 (1955).

[10]John Frank, Marble Palace: The Supreme Court in American Life, p. 6. Douglas objected to depleting a counselor's time. The Court Years 1939-1975, p. 180.

[11]Ibid., p. 101.

[12]Robert H. Jackson, "Advocacy Before the Supreme Court: Suggestions for Effective Case Presentation," 37 American Bar Association Journal, 803 (November, 1951).

[13]Anthony Lewis, Gideon's Trumpet, p. 163.

[14]John Marshall Harlan, "What Part Does the Oral Argument Play in the Conduct of an Appeal?" 41 Cornell Law Quarterly, 7 (1955).

[15]Arthur S. Miller and Jerome A. Barron, "The Supreme Court, the Adversary System, and the Flow of Information to the Justices," in Arthur Selyn Miller, The Supreme Court: Myth and Reality (Westport: Greenwood Press, 1978), p. 267. The Solicitor General as "repeat player" has an enormous advantage over the "one shotters." Doris Marie Provine, Case Selection in the United States Supreme Court, p. 91.

[16]Note, "Government Litigation in the Supreme Court: The Role of the Solicitor General," 78 Yale Law Journal, 1442 (1969).

[17]Kathryn Mickle Werdegar, "The Solicitor General and Administrative Due Process: A Quarter Century of Advocacy," 36 George Washington Law Review, 481 (1968).

[18]Anthony Lewis, "Our Extraordinary Solicitor General," The Reporter, May 5, 1955, p. 28. Steven Puro, "The United States as Amicus Curiae," in S. Sidney Ulmer (ed.) Courts, Law and Judicial Processes, p. 222, cites the frequent contacts between the President and Solicitor General, p. 222.

[19]Arthur Selyn Miller, "The Attorney General as the President's Lawyer," in Luther A. Huston et al, Roles of the Attorney General of the United States (Washington, D.C.: American Enterprise Institute, July, 1968), pp. 62-63.

[20]Simon E. Sobeloff, "Attorney for the Government. The Work of the Solicitor General's Office," 41 American Bar Association Journal, 230 (1955).

[21]Note, "Government Litigation in the Supreme Court: The Role of the Solicitor General," 78 Yale Law Journal 1456 (1969).

[22]Ibid., 1442 at 1465, note 103.

[23]Anthony Lewis, "Our Extraordinary Solicitor General," The Reporter, May 5, 1955, pp. 30-31. The case was Peters v. Hobby, 349 U.S. 331 (1955) that involved Dr. John P. Peters of the Yale University Medical School who was fired as a federal health consultant. The Loyalty Review Board had refused to tell him who were his accusers and to cross-examine them. Solicitor General Sobeloff believed it was a bad case, although the Government had won it below, and that Dr. Peters should have his job back.

[24]Simon E. Sobeloff, "Attorney For the Government. The Work of the Solicitor General's Office," 41 American Bar Association Journal, 230 (1955).

[25]Arthur Selyn Miller, "The Attorney General As the President's Lawyer," in Luther A. Huston et al, Roles of the Attorney General of the United States, p. 64.

[26]Kathryn Mickle Werdegar, "The Solicitor General and Administrative Due Process: A Quarter Century of Advocacy," 36 George Washington Law Review, 482 (1968).

[27]Note, "Government Litigation in the Supreme Court: The Role of the Solicitor General," 78 Yale Law Journal 1443 (1969).

[28]Kathryn Mickle Werdegar, "The Solicitor General and Administrative Due Process: A Quarter Century of Advocacy," p. 482. Those with petitioning expertise and experience tend to benefit from unclear standards of review and this, in turn, makes the federal government - represented by the Solicitor General "the principal beneficiary of the Court's secretive approach to case selection." Doris Marie Provine, Case Selection in the United States Supreme Court, p. 4, 45. "My analysis," further adds Provine, "points to one troubling feature in the current structure of case selection. In the Justices persistent campaign to maximize their discretion to select cases, they have given an advantage to sophisticated and experienced petitions, especially the United States government." Ibid., p. 175. See the several revealing charts and tables in Steven Puro, "The United States as Amicus Curiae" in S. Sidney Ulmer, Courts, Law and Judicial Processes that illustrate the kinds of cases the Solicitor General intervenes in and his high rate of success. pp. 223-237.

[29]Anthony Lewis, "Our Extraordinary Solicitor General," The Reporter, May 5, 1955, p. 27.

[30]Rule 42.3 Robert L. Stern and Eugene Gressman, Supreme Court Practice, p. 1104.

[31]Ibid., 749.

[32]Robert L. Stern, "The Solicitor General's Office and Administrative Agency Litigation," 46 American Bar Association Journal, 154-156 (February, 1960) reprinted in Joel B. Grossman and Richard S. Wells, Constitutional Law and Judicial Policy Making (New York: John Wiley & Sons, 1972), p. 193.

[33]Note, "Government Litigation in the Supreme Court: The Role of the Solicitor General," 78 Yale Law Journal 1445 (1969).

[34]Ibid., 1475.

[35]John Marshall Harlan, "What Part Does the Oral Argument Play in the Conduct of an Appeal?" 41 Cornell Law Quarterly 10 (1955). After complimenting the "star" advocates, both old and young, Justice Lewis Powell adds: "But the delight of the occasional high level of counsel performance is diluted by the more numerous performances that one must rate as 'average or poor' . . .. I certainly had expected that there would be relatively few mediocre performances before our Court. I regret to say that performance has not measured up to my expectations. Robert L. Stern and Eugene Gressman, Supreme Court Practice, pp. 732-733. When the oral arguments - often poorly presented and developed - became tedious, Justices Douglas and Frankfurter would exchange notes each teasing the other. William O. Douglas, The Court Years 1939-1975, p. 178.

[36]Note, "Government Litigation in the Supreme Court: The Role of the Solicitor General," 78 Yale Law Journal 1480 (1969). Lawyers in the Solicitor General's office have learned how to marshal their arguments to touch upon the Court's concerns and interests. "The absence of published standards of review-worthiness is not significant for these litigants. The lack of published standards . . . works to the advantage of (experienced) litigants . . . who project an image of competence and expertise . . .. Theirs will be the arguments read first and relied upon with least hesitation." Doris Marie Provine, Case Selection in the United States Supreme Court, p. 45. Also pp. 86, 87. Justice William O. Douglas calls attention to an almost intimate relationship between the Court and certain government agencies. The Court Years 1939-1975, p. 182.

[37]Incorporation is the legal concept under which the Supreme Court has "nationalized" the Bill of Rights, orginally believed to apply solely to the national government, and by means of the Fourteenth Amendment "transferred" these rights - minus several exceptions - to the states. Thus, if the Bill of Rights was binding on the national government, it was now binding on the state governments. Jack C. Plano and Milton Greenberg, The American Political Dictionary (New York: Holt, Rinehart and Winston, 1979), p. 73 has a very precise paragraph on "incorporation" and they assert that "the incorporation doctrine ranks among the most significant development in American Constitutional History." For a thorough discussion see John E. Nowak, Ronald D. Rotunda, and J. Nelson Young, Handbook on Constitutional Law (St. Paul: West Publishing Co., 1978), pp. 376-378, 410-419. In Barron v. Baltimore, 7 Peters 243 (1833), the Court held that the Bill of Rights limits only Congress. The Fourteenth Amendment (1868), section 1, says that no state shall abridge the privileges and immunities of United States citizens nor deprive any person of life, liberty, or property or equal protection of the law, without due process of law. As far as incorporation was concerned nothing much happened until 1925 when, seemingly out of the blue, the Court said in Gitlow v. New York, 268 U.S. 652 (1925): "For present purposes we may and do assume that freedom of speech and of the press - which are protected by the First Amendment from abridgment by Congress - are among the fundamental personal rights and "liberties" protected by the due process clause of the Fourteenth Amendment from impairment by the states." When, then, Florida allowed Gideon to go to jail without providing him a lawyer, had it erred? The Court said it had and thus "incorporated" such a right in Gideon v. Wainwright, 372 U.S. 335 (1963).

[38]Anthony Lewis, Gideon's Trumpet, p. 174.

[39]Ibid., 174.

[40]Ibid., 177.

[41]There have been seven former Attorneys General: Joseph McKenna (1898-1925) who served 26 years; William H. Moody (1906-1910) who served three years; James C. McReynolds (1914-1941) who served 26 years; Chief Justice Harlan F. Stone (1925-1941, 1941-1946) promoted as Chief Justice served twenty years; Frank Murphy (1940-1949) who served nine years; Robert H. Jackson (1941-1954) who served thirteen years; and Tom Clark (1949-1967) who served eighteen years. There have been two former Solicitors General, Stanley Reed (1937-1957) who served nineteen years and Thurgood Marshall (1967-) presently on the Court and has served thirteen years. One Deputy Atttorney General currently is on the Court, Byron White appointed in 1962 and Rehnquist and White also served as clerks, the former to Justice Robert H. Jackson and the latter to Chief Justice Fred Vinson. Justice John Paul Stevens served as a clerk to Justice Wiley Rutledge. "It would be difficult indeed," correctly note Blaustein and Mersky, "to single out any member of the Supreme Court who had not had important prior public service." Albert P. Blaustein and Roy M. Mersky. The First One Hundred Justices, 18. On the Justices "playing politics" or being "politicians" see Joseph F. Menez, "A Brief in Support of the Supreme Court," 54 Northwestern University Law Review, 33-36 (1959). Doris M. Provine noted that except for the Solicitor General's staff no sophisticated Supreme Court bar exists. Case Selection in the United States Supreme Court, p. 42. The writer suggests that there very much is such a bar consisting of all the additional "stars" that often, if not frequently, practice before the Court. Judges, like Presidents, have been "rated" by scholars and other Court watchers as Albert P. Blaustein and Roy M. Mersky point out in The First One Hundred Justices, pp. 32-51 and while there exists no ". . . foolproof formula . . . for selecting the best possible jurists" (p. 53) they do suggest a "failure" profile of a Supreme Court Justice (p. 69). See the rebuttal to this elitist argument by Everette E. Dennis, "Overcoming Occupational Heredity at the Supreme Court" 66 American Bar Association Journal, (January, 1980).

CHAPTER IX

THE AMICUS CURIAE: SOME MYTHS AND SOME REALITIES

It was not until the appearance of Henry Clay before the Court in 1821 that the Amicus curiae emerged.[1] It was more than 100 years later in 1937 that the amicus curiae was mentioned in the written rules of procedure. The increased use of amicus briefs today has taken on the appearance of group combat.[2] Especially was this true in 1950 when some 40 organizations filed briefs in the case involving The Hollywood Ten. The Communist Daily Worker even urged individuals to file "personal" briefs by writing letters to the Justices. Currently, amicus briefs, plus letters, telegrams, picketing and the like, are viewed as a formal part of lobbying.[3] Despite the Court's Rule 40, the use of briefs are all too often redundant and irrelevant[4] and are filed for strategy reasons as much as for elucidating the law.

The Justices tend to scrutinize amicus briefs less vigorously than they do principal briefs, and thus, a good deal of matter gets before the Court that would have been filtered or discarded in the trial court below. Professor Arthur Miller makes an excellent showing that many "facts" presented to the Court by way of amicus briefs are accepted although they did not run the gamut of the adversay process in the trial court. In fact, in not a few instances, matter was introduced into the Court this way that had never been part of the lower court record or that had not even been part of the principal briefs.[5] Arguments with little legal standing or of questionable legal doctrines which might irritate the Justices in the principal briefs are allowed in amicus briefs.

The amicus is best presented when the principal brief is adequately proffered, for it then performs a "valuable subsidiary role by introducing subtle variations of the basic argument, or emotive and even questionable arguments that might result in a successful verdict, but too risky to be embraced by the principal litigant."[6] On occasion the Court will deny an amicus brief. Two fresh instances involved an embarrassed Solicitor General[7] and the other a disappointed Black Caucus.[8] Recently, Chief Justice Warren Burger denounced from the Bench the filing of long amicus briefs. After chastizing counsel for submitting an amicus brief of

298 pages, he added: "I think you have done a service
to this Court. You have furnished Exhibit A why the
Court should activate a rule limiting briefs to 50 pages
unless the Court grants special leave."[9]

One reason the Court has not cracked down on this
growing burden and obvious lobbying of the Court is that
some Justices see this as an extension of the political
process. Another reason is that it allows the Justices
to gather new information that might normally be denied
them if they were restricted to the principal briefs.
Finally, the generous permission of amicus briefs allows
an activist, even a "non-activist" Court - as was the
Burger Court in the Abortion Cases - to act as a legislative committee and either to accept matter not decided
below in an adversarial manner or, in its oral argument,
to "state the argument they would like the petitioner
to make when counsel acting cautiously and constitutionally, have preferred more limited arguments."[10]

In United States v. Butler,[11] Justice Roberts laid
down a yardstick by which the Court determines the
constitutionality of an act of Congress. The Court has
only one duty, Roberts said, namely, "to lay the article
of the Constitution which is invoked beside the statue
which is challenged and to decide whether the latter
squares with the former." The trouble with that sim-
plistic view of decision making is that it was not true
when he announced it. It was, in fact, never true.
Whether the Supreme Court legislates, as some critics
claim, or fills in the interstices, it does more than
a mere mechanical operation. The law is not always
clear, and interpreting it is not always easy. The
Court does not follow the election returns as boldly
as Mr. Dooley[12] charged, but neither does it decide
cases in the same way a pharmicist prepares a remedy -
a little bit of this and a little bit of that, according
to some chemical formula.

It is difficult, if not impossible, to unravel the
"reasons" - what Justice Oliver W. Holmes called the
inarticulate major premise - for deciding a case this
way or that. More often than not the Justices themselves - except those with very distinct and precise
philosophies, and they have been few - do not know.
What is meant by a "judicial temperament," and how does
a Justice get it?[13] President A. Lawrence Lowell,
President of Harvard University, headed a distinguished
group of fifty-five Bostonians, including seven past
Presidents of the American Bar Association and testified:

"We do not believe that Mr. Brandeis has the judicial temperament and capacity which should be required in a judge of the Supreme Court."[14] Yet, in 1970 a distinguished panel of 65 law school deans and professors of law, history, and political science who deal with constitutional law rated the 100 Justices who have sat on the Supreme Court and placed Brandeis among "The Twelve Greatest."[15]

Does the appointment process give us a clue as to how a Justice will decide cases? Not with any degree of reliability. The President has one standard in appointing the Justice, the Senate has another in confirming him, and the American Bar Association, still another in rating his craftsmanship. Considering their longevity and the length of service, it is no wonder that Justices change - perhaps imperceptibly but change they do, nevertheless. Thus, Justice Blackmun a member of the "Minnesota Twins" - the other being Chief Justice Burger - despite viewing himself as a centrist has traveled in thirteen years from the conservative to the liberal wing. Stanley Reed started out as a liberal New Dealer, became a "swing" man and ultimately a conservative; and Chief Justice Charles E. Hughes traveled the same road but in the opposite direction. A liberal President, Woodrow Wilson appointed McReynolds who became a reactionary member of the Four Horseman, and Justice Frankfurter took a Harvard Law Professor's reputation and a tainted Sacco-Vanzetti image to the Court, and retired as a conservative and exponent of self-restraint. Thomas Jefferson urged President James Madison to appoint Joseph Story of Massachusetts, an intellectual great, to "neutralize" Chief Justice John Marshall, only to see Story "captured." More recently, Justice Black, the acknowledged leader of the Warren Court's liberal "bloc," pained his liberal followers by insisting that "free-speech" and "free-speech plus" were different. In the former, Congress, said Black, can make no law; but in the latter, the community can regulate "action."[16]

Does it make a difference if a Justice has had prior judicial experience? Justice Frankfurter[17] thought such experience of "zero" importance, and the record, in terms of the "Great" and "Near Great," bear him out. Every Justice possesses in different portions wisdom, energy, creativeness and persuasiveness - some, as Van Devanter, demonstrate it in conference, and some, as Hughes, in opinion writing; some are excellent craftsmen - lawyer's lawyers like John Marshall Harlan;

113

some, excellent writers, as Cardozo and Holmes; some, prolific and untidy, as Douglas; and some, like Brandeis, monkish and humble. All of the Justices however, have had the courage of their convictions, have judged as they knew how, sometimes cold-bloodedly and at other times humanely, but all have been attached to liberty, justice, freedom, dignity, and constitutionalism.

How a Justice votes, then is not all that easy to determine, scholarly and statistical studies often made to the contrary notwithstanding. What is meant by the "opinion" of the Court?[18] It depends. It depends on the vote margin, the points of agreement among the majority, the intensity of the concurrences, if any, and the shape of the dissent.

As respects the Court's adjudication of various issues, Justice Douglas quoted Lord Haldane who once remarked that you cannot study the work of the Judicial Committee of the Privy Council merely in the textbooks and documents: "The only way to study it is to watch it."[19] Similarly, before becoming a Supreme Court Justice, Felix Frankfurter regretted that "intimacies of the conference room - the workshop of the living constitution should be denied the historian."[20] This is why scholars, particularly political scientists, are Court-watchers, why they watch it function and study judicial behavior in decision-making. As long as the Court is not elected and, as contrasted with the political branches that are elected and accountable, it will be watched. In his Oliver Wendell Holmes lectures at Harvard, Judge Learned Hand said he was not about to be governed by a "bevy of Platonic Guardians."[21] One ready-made reason it is open to criticism is that except for the oral arguments, the work of the Court is largely secret. Perhaps its strength however is that, undisturbed by the electoral process or press review, it can deliberate, if not always calmly,[22] certainly boldly, about important constitutional matters. Puzzling but significant is that while the Court is undemocratic and less accountable than are the political branches, as to theory, it is the most popular, the most revered and the most constitutionally accepted of the three branches of the national government as to fact.

NOTES

CHAPTER IX

[1]Samuel Krislov, "The Amicus Curiae Brief: From Friendship
to Advocacy," 72 Yale Law Journal, 700 (1963).

[2]Glendon A. Schubert, Constitutional Politics: The Political
Behavior of Supreme Court Justices and the Constitutional Policies
That They Make (New York: Holt, Rinehart and Winston, 1960), p. 76.

[3]Samuel Krislov, "The Amicus Curiae Brief: From Friendship
to Advocacy," p. 72.

[4]Fowler V. Harper and Edwin D. Etherington, "Lobbyists Before
the Court," 101 University of Pennsylvania Law Review, 1172 (1953).
See also Nathan Hakman, "Lobbying the Supreme Court - An Appraisal
of Political Science Folklore," 35 Fordham Law Review 15-50 (1966)
reprinted in Sheldon Goldman and Austin Sarat, American Court
Systems: Readings in Judicial Process and Behavior, 216-230.

[5]Arthur Selyn Miller and Jerome A. Barron, "The Supreme
Court, the Adversary System, and the Flow of Information to the
Justices," in Arthur Selyn Miller, The Supreme Court: Myth and
Reality (Westport: Greenwood Press, 1978), pp. 270-271.

[6]Samuel Krislow, "The Amicus Curiae Brief: From Friendship
to Advocacy," 711.

[7]In United Airlines, Inc. v. McMann, 434 U.S. 192, 194
note 3 is the following: "No brief amicus was filed on behalf of
the Department of Labor in this Court, but after submission of the
case following oral argument the Solicitor General wrote a letter
to the clerk of this Court stating that the Government agreed with
the Fourth Circuit and was prepared to file amicus within three
weeks. The rules of this Court do not allow filing of briefs
amicus after oral argument. See Rule 42. No motion for leave to
file a brief amicus was filed." Chief Justice Warren Burger delivered this opinion which, surely, must have come as a surprise to
the Solicitor General.

[8]See 63 American Bar Association Journal, 1528 (November,
1977). The Congressional Black Caucus believed that the Government's brief to remand the case (to a lower court) would in the
view of Representative John Conyers (D. Mich.) ". . . encourage
the drowning of affirmative action in a tidal wave of litigation"
and result in "a major setback for civil rights."

[9]Peter W. Lewis and Kenneth D. People, The Supreme Court and the Criminal Process: Cases and Comments (Philadelphia: W. B. Saunders, 1978), p. 58.

[10]Arthur Selyn Miller and Jerome A. Barron, "The Supreme Court, the Adversary System, and the Flow of Information to the Justices," in Arthur Selyn Miller, The Supreme Court: Myth and Reality (Westport: Greenwood Press, 1978), p. 277.

[11]297 U.S. 1 (1936).

[12]Mr. Dooley, the American humorist, was, of course, Finley Peter Dunne (1867-1936) whose special forte was his style as much as his wit. The full quotation reads: "No matter whether th' constitution follows th' flag or not, th' supreme court follows th' iliction returns." John Bartlett, Bartlett's Familiar Quotations (14th ed. Rev. 7 enlarged. Boston: Little, Brown, 1968), p. 890. For a capsule but precise biography of Finley Peter Dunne, see Charles Van Doren and Robert McHenry, Webster's American Biographies (Springfield: G. and C. Merriam Co., 1975), p. 298. What Dooley was referring to, of course, is what is known historically as the Insular Cases (Dorr v. United States, 195 U.S. 138 (1905); Downes v. Bidwell, 182 U.S. 244 (1901); and Hawaii v. Mankichi, 190 U.S. 197 (1903) in which the Court declared that the Constitution did not follow the flag, that is to say, the rights of United States citizens did not automatically belong to the people of overseas territories. The Court suggested that the fundamental rights guaranteed by the Constitution applied but not the formal ones. See, however, the Court's most recent views on America's possessions, notably, Puerto Rico in Torres v. Puerto Rico, 61 L. Ed. 2d 1 (1979) in which it was held that the Fourth Amendment's guarantee of unreasonable searches and seizures was applicable and that Puerto Rico could not act, just as the other states of the Union could not act as though it was a sovereign state for international relations purposes and thus free of the Bill of Rights.

[13]Joseph F. Menez, "Whose Judicial Temperament?" Commonweal, April 10, 1959, p. 51.

[14]Alpheus Thomas Mason, Brandeis: A Free Man's Life (New York: Viking Press, 1946), p. 472.

[15]Albert P. Blaustein and Roy M. Mersky, The First One Hundred Justices, p. 37.

[16]Hugo L. Black, A Constitutional Faith (New York: Knopf, 1969), p. 63.

[17]Felix Frankfurter, "The Supreme Court in the Mirror of Justices," 105 University of Pennsylvania Law Review, 781 (1957) reprinted in Walter F. Murphy and C. Herman Pritchett, Courts, Judges, and Politics, pp. 178-180.

[18]If an opinion of the Court commands a majority of partici- pating judges, it becomes the "opinion of the Court." When a majority of the Justices agree on a result but not the rationale and this results in four Justices or less then the opinion is referred to as a "plurality opinion" of Mr. Justice so-and-so. The "plurality opinion" is usually not regarded as precedential. In addition to joining a majority, one or more Justices might write a concurring opinion. "Opinions of the Court' are usually signed but occasionally a per curiam opinion is unsigned. It has no more and no less force than one which is signed. The per curiam opinion is often used in cases easily resolved, and extremely brief, and have been disposed of without oral argument. See William Cohen and John Kaplan, Bill of Rights (Mineola: The Foundation Press, 1976), p. 67 note 79. Joel B. Grossman and Richard S. Wells, Constitutional Law and Judicial Policy Making (New York: Wiley and Sons, 1972), p. 50. See also the stinging rebuke of Justice Stevens, dissenting, in which he protests the increasing use of per curiam opinions and also the use of the Court to correct errors below. Board of Education of Rogers, Arkansas v. McCluskey, 73 L. Ed. 2d 1273 and 1279 (1982). On rare occasions the Court will decide an orally argued case by way of a per curiam opinion, such as the Pentagon Papers controversy in 1971 (The New York Times v. United States, 403 U.S. 713) and the Federal Election Campaign Act determining the constitutionality of public financing of presidential nominating conventions and primary campaigns, Buckley v. Valeo, 424 U.S. 1 (1976). In Buckley five of the eight Justices that participated wrote separate opin- ions and with the appendix covered in excess of 100 pages; in New York Times, the per curiam opinion covered three paragraphs. See Harold J. Spaeth, Supreme Court Policy Making, p. 27 note. Finally, when no majority results (as it did eight times in the 1976-77 Term of the Court) the prevailing opinion is labeled the "Judgment of the Court" which provides little guidance and has little precedential value. Ibid., 28 note. See James Y. Carter v. Luther Miller, 54 L. Ed. 2d 603 (1978). In a bitterly divided case in which Justice Brennan announced the judgment of the Court the holding that a school board could not remove certain books from the Junior high school and high school libraries, Chief Justice Burger, dissenting, wrote: ". . . the plurality expresses views on a very important constitutional issue. Fortunately, there is no binding holding of the Court on the critical constitutional issue presented." Board of Education v. Pico, 23 L. Ed. 2d 435, 459 n. 2 (1982).

[19]William O. Douglas, "The Supreme Court and Its Caseload,"45 Cornell Law Quarterly, 414 (1960).

[20]Alpheus Thomas Mason, "Myth and Reality in Supreme Court Decisions," 48 Virginia Law Review 1405, note 105 (1962). Alan B. Morrison believes there are a number of ways to democratise the Court short of impairing its decision-making process. Thus he advocates (a) the televising of oral arguments (parenthetically, it might be noted that the Court supports televised state trials – Chandler v. Florida, 66 L. Ed. 2d 740 (1981); (b) streamlining the system under which reporters get the Court's opinions which are distributed now at the time orally delivered; (c) publishing the "dead list" so that lawyers could prepare future cases more adequately, save clients a fruitless expense, and cut down on appeals; (d) distributing the public papers of the Justices, especially of the Chief Justice since there is no depository today; (e) reviewing the current practice of recusals to see if the law on disqualification is sensible. A four-four tie due to disqualification, without opinion, affirms a decision below is faulty and does less than justice to the litigant; (f) altering the practice by which the Court changes its rules without any explanation; (g) and, finally, divising a system, without invading a Justice's privacy or independence, of knowing whether he is medically fit to serve. "The Brethren: Focusing on the Wrong Secrecy" 66 American Bar Association Journal, 563-566 (May, 1980). Many of Morrison's criticisms are countered and dismissed by Barrett McGurn, former public information officer of the Court, 1973-1982 in "Public Information at the United States Supreme Court," 69 American Bar Association Journal, 40-45 (January, 1983). In a swift and exceedingly strong rebuttal to Barrett McGurn, in turn, Gilbert Cranberg, formerly editorial page writer of the Des Moines Register claims that while the Court appears to be open "secrecy pervades the highest court more than is necessary or healthy in a society whose institutions of justice must be accountable to the public." Along with other points, Cranberg charges that (a) the Justices veil "in secrecy their own compliance with law" that is, conflict of interest; (b) the Justices, specifically Lewis Powell and Potter Stewart, did not recuse themselves in some cases involving a denial of certiorari, despite financial interests; (c) and, finally, secret recusal is counter to the spirit and purpose of the disqualification statute and the code of criminal conduct. "A Court of Supreme Secrecy," 69 American Bar Association Journal, 622-623 (May, 1983).

[21]Learned Hand, The Bill of Rights (Cambridge: Harvard University Press, 1958), p. 73.

[22]The Justices seem to be losing their cool as opinions show unusual signs of acrimony. In addition, comments on and off the bench have become common and pointed. Stephen Wermiel, "Low - Roading on the High Court," The Wall Street Journal, September 13, 1982 (editorial page).

A SHORT LIST OF BOOKS ON THE SUPREME COURT

Abraham, Henry J.   The Judiciary: The Supreme Court in the
Governmental Process 3rd ed. (Boston: Allyn
& Bacon, 1973)

"   ,   "   ".   The Judicial Process (Oxford University
Press, 1975)

Acheson, D. C.   The Supreme Court: America's Judicial
Heritage (Dodd, Mead, 1961)

Asch, S. H.   The Supreme Court and Its Great Justices
(Arco, 1971)

Baker, Leonard   John Marshall. A Life in Law (Macmillan,
1974)

Ball, Howard   Courts and Politics: The Federal Judicial
System (Prentice Hall, 1980)

Barth, Alan   Prophets With Honor: Great Dissents and Great
Dissenters in the Supreme Court (Random
House, 1974)

Berger, Raoul   Congress Versus Supreme Court (Harvard University Press, 1969)

"   ,   "   Government By Judiciary (Harvard University
Press, 1977)

Baum, Lawrence   The Supreme Court (Congressional Quarterly
Press, 1981)

Berkson, Larry   The Supreme Court and its Publics; the
Communication of Policy Decisions (Lexington,
1978)

Bickel, Alexander M.   The Least Dangerous Branch: The Supreme
Court at the Bar of Politics (Bobbs-Merrill,
1963)

"   ,   "   ".   The Supreme Court and the Idea of Progress
(Harper & Row, 1970)

Blaustein, Albert P.   The First One Hundred Justices, Statistical
& Roy M. Mersky   Studies on the Supreme Court of the United
States (Archon Books, 1978)

Bowen, Catherine D.   Yankee from Olympus (Little, Brown, 1945)

Choper, Jesse H. <u>Judicial Review and the National Political Process. A Function Reconsideration of the Role of the Supreme Court</u>

Congressional <u>Guide to the U.S. Supreme Court</u> (Congress-
Quarterly ional Quarterly, Inc., 1979)

Cox, Archibald <u>The Role of the Supreme Court in American Government</u> (Oxford, 1976)

Danelski, David <u>A Supreme Court Justice is Appointed</u> (Random House, 1964)

Ducat, Craig R. <u>Modes of Constitutional Interpretation</u> (West Publishing Co., 1978)

Dunham, Allison & <u>Mr. Justice</u> (University of Chicago Press,
Philip B. Kurland 1964)

Ely, John Hart <u>Democracy and Distrust: A Theory of Judicial Review</u> (Harvard University Press, 1980)

Ernest, M. L. <u>The Great Reversals: Tales of the Supreme Court</u> (Weybright and Tallery, 1973)

Fisher, Louis <u>The Constitution Between Friends: Congress, President, and the Law</u> (St. Martin's Press, 1978)

Frank, John P. <u>Marble Palace: The Supreme Court in American Life</u> (Knopf, 1958)

Freund, P. A. <u>On Understanding the Supreme Court: Its Business, Purposes, and Performance</u> (Meridian, 1961)

Funston, Richard <u>A Vital National Seminar: The Supreme Court in American Political Life</u> (Mayfield, 1978)

Goldberg, Arthur J. <u>Equal Justice: The Warren Era of the Supreme Court</u> (Northwestern University Press, 1971)

Goldman, S. & <u>The Federal Courts as a Political System</u> (Harper & Row, 1971)

Horowitz, Donald L. <u>The Courts and Social Policy</u> (Brookings Institution, 1977)

Kelly, Alfred,
Winfred A. Harbison,
& Herman Belz

The American Constitution Its Origins and Development 1789-1982 (W. W. Norton & Co., 1983)

Kolmeier, L. M.

"God Save This Honorable Court!" (Scribners, 1973)

Krislov, Samuel

The Supreme Court in the Political Process (Macmillan, 1965)

Kurland, Philip B.

Politics, the Constitution, and the Warren Court (University of Chicago Press, 1973)

Lewis, Anthony

Gideon's Trumpet (Random House, 1960)

Magrath, C. Peter

Morris R. Waite: The Triumph of Character (Macmillan, 1963)

Mason, Alpheus T.

William Howard Taft - Chief Justice (Simon & Schuster, 1965)

" ,   "   ".

Harlan Fiske Stone, Pillar of the Law (Viking Press, 1956)

" ,   "   ".

The Supreme Court from Taft to Burger (Louisiana State University Press, 1979)

Murphy, Bruce

The Brandeis-Frankfurter Connection (Oxford University Press, 1982)

Murphy, Walter F.

Elements of Judicial Strategy (University of Chicago Press, 1973)

Murphy, Paul L.

The Constitution in Crisis Times 1918-1939 (Harper & Row, 1972)

Rohde, David W. &
Harold J. Spaeth

Supreme Court Decision Making (Freeman, 1976)

Provine, Doris Marie

Case Selection in the United States Supreme Court (University of Chicago Press, 1980)

Schmidhauser, John R.

Judges and Justices: The Federal Appellate Judiciary (Little, Brown and Co., 1979)

"   ,   "   ".

The Supreme Court: Its Politics, Personalities, and Procedures (Hold, 1960)

Scigliano, R.

The Supreme Court and the Presidency (Free Press, 1972)

Simon, James F.   Independent Journey: The Life of William O.
                         Douglas (Penguin Books, 1983)

Spaeth, Harold J.   Supreme Court Policy Making: Explanation and
                         Prediction (Freeman, 1979)

Stern, Robert C. &   Supreme Court Procedure. 5th ed. (Bureau of
Eugene Gressman   National Affairs, 1978)

Tribe, Lawrence   American Constitutional Law (Foundation
                         Press, 1978)

Wasby, Stephen L.   Continuity and Change: From Warren Court to
                         the Burger Court (Goodyear, 1976)

Westin, Alan F.   The Supreme Court: Views From Inside (W. W.
                         Norton, 1961)

White, G. Edward   The American Judicial Tradition: Profiles
                         of Leading American Judges (Oxford Uni-
                         versity Press, 1978)

 " , ".   "   Earl Warren: A Public Life (Oxford Uni-
                         versity Press, 1982)

Wilkinson, J. Harvie   Serving Justice: A Supreme Court Clerk's
III   View (Charterhouse, 1974)

Woodford, Howard J.   Mr. Justice Murphy: A Political Biography
                         (Princeton University Press, 1968)

Members of the United States Supreme Court
1789-1983

Name	State & Party	Appointed by	Replaced	Years Served
John Jay	N.Y.(F)	Washington		1789-1795
John Rutledge	S.C.(F)	"		1789-1791
William Cushing	Ma.(F)	"		1789-1791
James Wilson	Pa.(F)	"		1789-1798
John Blair	Va.(F)	"		1789-1796
James Iredell	N.C.(F)	"	Harrison	1790-1799
Thomas Johnson	Md.(F)	"	Ruthledge	1791-1793
Wm. Patterson	N.J.(F)	"	Johnson	1793-1806
John Rutledge (1)	S.C.(F)	"	Jay	
Samuel Chase	Md.(F)	"	Blair	1796-1811
O. Ellsworth	Conn.(F)	"	Jay	1796-1800
B. Washington	Va.(F)	Adams	Wilson	1798-1829
Alfred Moore	N.C.(F)	"	Iredell	1799-1804
John Marshall	Va.(F)	"	Ellsworth	1801-1835
Wm. Johnson	S.C.(D-R)	Jefferson	Moore	1804-1834
H.B. Livingston	N.Y.(D-R)	"	Patterson	1806-1823
Thomas Todd	Ky.(D.R.)	"		1807-1826
Joseph Story	Ma.(D.R.)	Madison	Cushing	1811-1845
Gabriel Duval	Md.(D.R.)	"	Chase	1811-1835
Smith Thompson	N.Y.(D.R.)	Monroe	Livingston	1823-1843
Robert Trimble	Ky.(D.R.)	J.Q.Adams	Todd	1826-1828
John McLean	Ohio(D)	Jackson	Trimble	1829-1861
Henry Baldwin	Pa.(D)	"	Washington	1830-1844
James M. Wayne	Ga.(D)	"	Johnson	1835-1867
Roger B. Taney	Md.(D)	"	Marshall	1836-1864
P. P. Babour	Va.(D)	"	Duval	1836-1841
John Catron	Tenn.(D)			1837-1865
John McKinley	Ala.(D)	Van Buren		1837-1852
Peter V. Daniel	Va.(D)	"	Barbour	1841-1860
Samuel Nelson	N.Y.(D)	Tyler	Thompson	1845-1872
Levi Woodbury	N.H.(D)	Polk	Story	1845-1851
Robert C. Grier	Pa.(D)	"	Baldwin	1846-1870
Ben. R. Curtis	Ma.(W)	Fillmore	Woodbury	1851-1857
John A. Campbell	Ala.(D)	Pierce	McKinley	1853-1861
Nathan Clifford	Ma.(D)	Buchanan	Curtis	1858-1881
Noah H. Swayne	Ohio(R)	Lincoln	McLean	1862-1881
Samuel F. Miller	Iowa(R)	"	Daniel	1862-1890
David Davis	Ill.(R)	"	Campbell	1862-1877
S. J. Field	Ca.(D)	"		1863-1897
Salmon P. Chase	Ohio(R)	"	Taney	1864-1873
William Strong	Pa.(R)	Grant	Grier	1870-1880
Joseph P. Bradley	N.J.(R)	"		1870-1892
Ward Hunt	N.Y.(R)	"	Nelson	1872-1882
Morrison Waite	Ohio(R)	"	Chase	1874-1888
J. M. Harlan	Ky.(R)	Hayes	Davis	1877-1911

Name	State & Party	Appointed by	Replaced	Years Served
Wm. B. Woods	Ga.(R)	Hayes	Strong	1880-1887
Stan. Mathews	Ohio(R)	"	Swayne	1881-1889
Horace Gray	Ma.(R)	Arthur	Clifford	1881-1902
Sam. Blatchford	N.Y.(R)	"	Hunt	1882-1893
Lucius Q.C. Lamar	Miss.(D)	Cleveland	Woods	1888-1893
M. W. Fuller	Ill.(D)	Cleveland	Waite	1888-1910
David Brewer	Kan.(R)	Harrison	Mathews	1889-1910
Henry B. Brown	Mich.(R)	"	Miller	1890-1906
George Shiras	Pa.(R)	"	Bradley	1892-1903
H. E. Jackson	Tenn.(D)	"	Lamar	1893-1895
Edward D. White(2)	La.(D)	Cleveland	Blatchford	1894-1910
R. W. Peckham	N.Y.(D)	"	Jackson	1895-1909
Joseph McKenna	Ca.(R)	McKinley	Field	1898-1925
O. W. Holmes,Jr.	Ma.(R)	Roosevelt	Gray	1902-1932
William R. Day	Ohio(R)	"	Shiras	1903-1922
Wm. H. Moody	Ma.(R)	"	Brown	1906-1910
Horace Lurton	Tenn.(D)	Taft	Packham	1909-1914
Edward D. White	La.(D)	"	Fuller	1910-1921
Charles E. Hughes(2)	N.Y.(R)	"	Brewer	1910-1916
W.Van Devanter	Wyo.(R)	"	Moody	1910-1937
Joseph Lamar	Ga.(D)	"	White	1910-1916
Mahlon Pitney	N.J.(R)	"	Harlan	1912-1922
J.C. McReynolds	Tenn.(D)	Wilson	Lurton	1914-1940
Louis Brandeis	Ma.(R)	"	Lamar	1916-1939
John H. Clarke	Ohio(D)	"	Hughes	1916-1922
William H. Taft	Conn.(R)	Harding	White	1921-1930
G. Sutherland	Utah(R)	"	Clarke	1922-1938
Pierce Butler	Minn.(D)	"	Day	1922-1939
E. T. Sanford	Tenn.(R)	"	Pitney	1923-1930
Harlan F. Stone(2)	N.Y.(R)	Coolidge	McKenna	1925-1941
Charles E. Hughes	N.Y.(R)	Hoover	Taft	1930-1941
Owen J. Roberts	Pa.(R)	"	Sanford	1930-1945
Ben. N. Cardozo	N.Y.(D)	"	Holmes	1932-1938
Hugo L. Black	Ala.(D)	Roosevelt	VanDevanter	1937-1971
Stanley F. Reed	Ky.(D)	"	Sutherland	1938-1957
Felix Frankfurter	Ma.(I)	"	Cardozo	1939-1962
Wm. O. Douglas	Conn.(D)	"	Brandeis	1939-1975
Frank Murphy	Mich.(D)	"	Butler	1940-1949
Harlan F. Stone	N.Y.(R)	"	Hughes	1941-1946
James. F. Byrnes	S.C.(D)	"	Stone	1941-1942
Robert H. Jackson	N.Y.(D)	"	McReynolds	1941-1954
W. B. Rutledge	Iowa(D)	"	Byrnes	1943-1949
Harold Burton	Ohio(R)	Truman	Roberts	1945-1958
Fred M. Vinson	Ky.(D)	"	Stone	1946-1953
Tom C. Clark	Texas(D)	"	Murphy	1949-1967
Sherman Minton	Ind.(D)	"	Ruthledge	1949-1956
Earl Warren	Ca.(R)	Eisenhower	Vinson	1953-1969

Name	State & Party	Appointed by	Replaced	Years Served
John M. Harlan (2)	N.Y.(R)	Eisenhower	Jackson	1955-1971
W. J. Brennan, Jr.	N.J.(D)	"	Minton	1956-
C. E. Whittaker	Mo.(R)	"	Reed	1957-1962
Potter Stewart	Ohio(R)	"	Burton	1958-1981
Byron R. White	Colo.(D)	Kennedy	Whittaker	1962-
A. J. Goldberg	Ill.(D)	"	Frankfurter	1962-1965
Abe Fortas (3)	Tenn(D)	Johnson	Goldberg	1965-1969
Thurgood Marshall	N.Y.(D)	"	Clark	1967-
Warren Burger	Minn.(R)	Nixon	Warren	1969-
Harry Blackmun	Minn.(R)	Nizon	Fortas	1970
Lewis F. Powell	Va.(D)	"	Black	1972-
Wm. Rehnquist	Ariz.(R)	"	Harlan	1972-
John P. Stevens	Ill.(R)	Ford	Douglas	1975-
Sandra O'Connor	Ariz.(R)	Reagan	Stewart	1981-

Letter after state signify as follows:
F   Federalist
D   Democrat
R   Republican
W   Whig
I   Independent
D-R Democrat-Republican

The name of the Chief Justice is underlined

Number after a justice signifies as follows:
(1)   Unconfirmed
(2)   First sat as Associate Justice
(3)   Rejected as Chief Justice

Fein, Bruce 75.

Field, Justice Stephen J. 72.

Ford, Pres. Gerald 54.

Fortas, Justice Abe 50, 55, 57,
58, 59, 100, 103, 105, 106.

Frank, John P. 30, 34, 42, 56,
57, 67, 72, 75, 76, 78, 85,
91, 94, 95, 106.

Frankfurter, Justice Felix 1,
5, 12, 22, 23, 36, 37, 38,
59, 64, 67, 68, 69, 71, 76,
77, 80, 84, 85, 87, 88, 89,
100, 108, 113, 114, 117.

Freund, Paul A. 6, 15, 17, 18,
33.

Friedman, Leon 10, 44, 53, 54,
56, 57, 59, 71.

Fuller, Chief Justice M. 47,
63, 77.

Funston, Richard Y. 95.

Galbraith, John Kenneth 55.

Garraty, John A. 59.

Goldberg, Justice Arthur 5, 11,
55.

Goldman, S. (& Sarat) 13, 14,
67, 115.

Goldman, S. (& Jahnige) 12, 13,
57, 69, 70, 83, 86, 87.

Gravel, Senator Mike 36.

Gray, Justice Horace 33.

Greenhouse, Linda 16, 19, 95.

Gressman, Eugene 13, 25, 30.

Griswold, Erwin N. 9, 13, 16, 18.

Grossman, Joel B. 57, 88, 108.

Grossman, Joel B. (& Wells) 28,
57, 76, 117.

Gunther, Gerald 12, 16, 33.

Haines, Charles Grove 70.

Hakman, Nathan 115.

Haldane, Lord J. B. S. 114.

Haldeman, H. R. (Bob) 24.

Halpern, Stephen C. 10.

Hamilton, Alexander 1.

Hand, Judge Learned 114, 118.

Harlan, Justice John M. (2) 2,
23, 38, 79, 80, 84, 96, 99,
100, 105, 106, 108, 113.

Harlan, Justice John M. (1) 78,
89, 90.

Harper, Fowler V. 87, 115.

Harrell, Mary Ann 10, 29, 41,
73, 85.

Harris, II, William F. 97.

Hart, Jr., Henry M. 91, 95.

Hayes, Pres. Rutherford B. 59.

Hayes-Tilden Election 59.

Hazard, Geoffrey C. 12.

Holmes, Justice O. W. 1, 4, 15,
47, 74, 77, 89, 92, 96, 111,
114.

Hoover, Pres. Herbert 47, 54,
101.

Tocqueville, Alexis de 69.

Totenberg, Nina 6, 14, 18, 24, 27, 42, 69, 71, 87, 97.

Tribe, Laurence 31.

Trimble, Bruce R. 70, 74, 75.

Truman, Harry S. 36, 44, 50, 51, 53, 56, 59.

Ulmer, S. Sidney 11, 12, 19, 68, 70, 71, 72, 76, 84, 85, 93, 107, 108.

Van Devanter, Justice Willis 54, 57, 64, 71, 74, 113.

Van Doren, Charles (& McHenry) 55, 105, 116.

Vinson, Chief Justice Fred 33, 36, 42, 44, 49, 50, 51, 53, 110.

Viorst, Milton 95.

Voorhees, Theodore 4, 15, 74.

Waite, Chief Justice Morris 29, 47, 68, 70, 72, 74, 75.

Warren Commission 59.

Warren Court 4, 6, 71, 91, 96.

Warren, Chief Justice Earl 2, 4, 5, 6, 10, 25, 31, 50, 51, 56, 59, 61, 63, 67, 68, 70, 96, 100, 105.

Wasby, Stephen L. 55.

Wiermiel, Stephen 17, 43, 118.

Webster, Daniel 99.

Werdegar, Kathryn Mickle 107, 108.

Weston, Alan 83, 85, 86.

White, Justice Byron 4, 5, 12, 21, 24, 42, 110.

White, Edward 15, 43, 44, 53, 55, 56, 59, 62, 67, 70, 71, 72, 74, 94.

White, Chief Justice Edward 48.

White, William 55.

Whittaker, Justice Charles 83, 96.

Wildavsky, Aaron (& Polsby) 42, 72, 94, 97.

Wilkinson, J. Harvie 41, 42, 85.

Williams, Richard L. 14, 17, 19, 42, 67.

Wilson, Woodrow 47, 48, 53, 56, 91, 113.

Woodward, Bob (& Armstrong) 30.

Young, Rowland L. 84.

THE AUTHOR

Dr. Joseph F. Menez attended Harvard University and the University of Notre Dame where he received a Ph.D. in Political Science in 1952. He taught at the University of Detroit, Loyola University-Chicago, where he was chairman of the Department of Political Science for four years, and since 1968 has taught in the Department of Political Science at Ball State University, Muncie, Indiana. His specialty is Constitutional Law. He was a John F. O'Hara Fellow at Notre Dame 1950, Faculty Man of the Year 1964 at Loyola University, and in 1960-61 was a Smith-Mundt Senior Lecturer in American Politics to the National Universities of Peru. Dr. Menez has taught overseas at the Loyola University Rome Center, and at United States Air Force Bases in Spain and Germany. In 1976 he delivered a series of Lectures on Constitutional Law in Taiwan. At one time or another, he has lectured at Marquette University, Mundelein College-Chicago, St. Louis University, John Carroll University-Cleveland, Notre Dame University, Miami-Dade Junior College, Biscayne College-Miami, the University of Lisbon, Inter-American University, San Gernan, Puerto Rico, the University of Puerto Rico. Versatile in Spanish and Portuguese, Dr. Menez has also lectured in Spain and Portugal. A regular book and manuscript reviewer, Dr. Menez has contributed to such scholarly journals as Mid-America, The Critic, Commonweal, Social Science, Anthropos, The Midwest Journal of Political Science, South Atlantic Quarterly, Northwestern University Law Review and Queen's Quarterly. With Paul C. Bartholomew, Dr. Menez has co-authored Summaries of Leading Cases on the Constitution, 12th edition (1983).